How To Fight A Pig

How To Fight A Pig

The journey I took in filing a 1983 Lawsuit against the City of Phoenix in 2018. Representing myself with no attorney, also known as Pro Se

DAVID CHATWOOD

How To Fight A Pig

Disclaimer

Although the content provided in this book is a great resource, it is provided with the understanding that neither the author nor the publisher is engaged in presenting specific legal advice. Individuals who have had their rights violated should engage with a licensed, qualified attorney or other competent professional.

Author: David Chatwood

Photo: Wavy Folio Photography 2023 ©

MERICA

Contents

Introduction

A former songwriter and aspiring comedian stopped to check on a car accident in Phoenix, AZ. Next thing you know, he's staring at the concrete in handcuffs.

"Knees weak, palms are sweaty on the surface; you look calm, but you keep forgetting." We have rights. As his former rap group members are locked up for pushing P.

D-Wood goes to the law library and pushes PTSD. Laugh and learn how D-Wood won a 1983 Excessive force lawsuit settlement without a lawyer or money.

This piece is a true story of how he used the law to manifest enough money to keep him on his spiritual journey. No one needs to know how to fight a good cop because you won't have to. But everyone needs to know how to fight a Pig. A jewel for single moms to gain insight into why some fathers discipline their sons in the manner they do. It is one thing to protect them, but it is another thing to prepare them for the harsh realities of this world.

EntraproNegroes On the Rise

Kan't N.O.C. Records Inc.

Lava Boiz

DJ Jax
Nev
H
H

IF YOU SEE DA POLICE

WARN A BROTHER

Chapter One

IF YOU SEE DA POLICE WARN A BROTHER

Inside a pitch-black closet, a device lights up, and a T mobile Sidekick 3 pops up on a screen. A hand clicks to receive an AOL instant message.

How's Phoenix? A message from Angie pops on the screen.

Caramel fingers with hairy knuckles type a response.

As a kid, I always wanted to go in the dryer, but I was afraid I'd get stuck there. Now, every day is a permanent press; won't he do it?

An apartment door swings open, and a young dark-skinned man wearing a NY baseball hat and streetwear enters, looking like he just walked on stage to his concert. He raps into a paper sack like a microphone. Three young women wearing red and purple skirts with matching lipstick follow him like a Conga line into the apartment.

"Bitches and Bacardi

It's still a party

Where da innocent hoes get naughty

And ya fa sure to find a hottie

Widda a body

Why's that dog?

Bitches and Bacardi."

"Let's Go!" says a taller dark-skinned man vibing to their entrance.

"Really?" says a muffled voice.

With a finger to his mouth, the man pulls the bottle from the paper sack and bangs it on the closet door.

Knock knock knock,

"Bless the bottle, Pedro!" says the man as an instrumental beat is turned up.

The closet door swings open, and a caramel-colored hand reaches out, making a cross sign over the bottle.

"He got a sidekick, girl, he got a sidekick," two of the girls sing in unison, gyrating. The door closes gently before being pushed open again.

"I gotta sidekick. I'm lookin for a side chick," says the caramel-colored man wearing a muscle shirt and holding up his T-Mobile Sidekick,

"Ooooowwwwwe," says Larry Wayne

"I gotta sidekick. I'm lookin for a side chick."

"Ayyye," yells the girls.

"I gotta sidekick. I'm lookin for a side chick."

Larry starts rapping and dancing behind the girl in purple.

"Who is in that purple? I'm creepin up on her. Why she throw it in a circle?"

D-Wood starts rapping while walking toward the other girl.

"You chose purple. Ama choose red. I see it in her eyes that she wanna give me... "

He raises his hand to the girl in red's face as if it were a microphone.

"Head," says the girl in red

"Ayyyyye," they all start laughing

"Dat's what I'm talkin bout my bitch got barz, ha-haha," said the girl in purple.

"I shaved my balls, but they back hairy. The other black guy raps, "I'll take yo side chick with my BlackBerry, hahaha," as he puts his hand on one of the girls, and they all laugh.

"Larry, let me roll this," her long purple diamond studded nails push a small pile of marijuana off a magazine onto the kitchen counter.

"If You See Da Police, Warn A Brotha," she reads while staring at the magazine's cover.

"Is this y'all?"

"Yeah, I told you they be doin them thug dizzle!" says a dark-skinned girl pulling the blonde girl's face towards hers.

"Shotgun hoe," their succulent purple and red lips inched closer together. Like in "The Lady and the Tramp," they shared a noodle-like stream of smoke directly from one girl's lips to the other.

"Khoff Khak Khak," the blonde coughed as her lungs could take no more. Satisfied, the black girl opened her mouth and removed the lighted blunt she had placed in her mouth in the opposite direction.

The other Caucasian girl grabs a bottle of baby powder from a counter.

"What's this for?"

Larry opens his hand, signaling for her to pour some into his palm.

"More," he says, opening his palms excited.

The other man flashes a devilish smile.

"You sure you wanna-?"

'Poof,' an explosion of white powder filled the room, bouncing off the girl's face like pizza dough in a bowl of flour.

"Motherfu-," she says, reaching for him as he jumps back, avoiding her hands.

Gagging and laughing, they waved their ghostly hands through the blizzard of baby powder and marijuana.

"Talk while someone's in the booth; you get the powda," says Larry Wayne, smiling like the joker.

"D-Wood, what's good? You ready?"

"Nah, I just love being in the closet," said a muffled voice.

"You said it, not me," he replied, holding back laughter.

He grabs the mouse and clicks the record button.

Sweat dripped down D-Wood's chiseled chest inside the closet. His head swayed back and forth rhythmically as the instrumental played through his headphones. He approached the microphone with confidence.

"This ain't nothin but therapy in the booth

It's like everywhere I gooooo

lizards is extra hatin

Every time I come home

My chick wanna an explanation

How many hoes you got?

What's the estimation?

Get out my business biiiitch!

Escalamation

I'm just a bruva from KC

Misplaced in AZ

Kinfolk was bout to raise me

Pops came through bout age three

That's only page three

I'm a mu-phuckin animal

Meet me at cage three

Yeah, no momma just substitutes

And if they ain't had no loot

Pops'll treat em like prostitutes

Swung on me so much

Now I can duke

And if I hit you in ya stomach

You will say

I can puke

Yeah yeah, you ain't gon wanna fight

You gon say

I can shoot

Ama be like lil duffle bag boy I rebuke

I ain't the bomb

I'm the Nuke

Nothin small

Nothin Cute

This ain't nothin but therapy in the booth!

If a hater talkin shit to you

You MAN UP MAN UP

Steady stackin paper

Get your GRANDS UP GRANDS UP

Actin like you down

You better STAND UP STAND UP

We ain't scared to leave this bitch in

HAND CUFFS, HAND CUFFS."

Chapter Two

REAL EYES REALIZE REAL LIES

(Five years later)

Eyes closed, ED-Wood sits in the driver's seat of a car. His cell phone plays a video recording of a man speaking.

"The Universe wants me to live a rich and abundant life, and it will support me in making this a reality," said an elderly man's voice.

He knocks his shoes off and brings his feet together like pray hands.

A phone call interrupts the recording.

"You have a collect call from Larry Wayne. Press one to accept this call or press two to disconnect," says an operator's voice.

"Larry Wizzle, what's poppin?"

"What's good?"

"Nigga, we never had a chance!"

"What you mean?"

D-Wood flicks a bic and lights a half-smoked joint.

"I'm listenin to this Bob Proctor dude,"

"That's my guy."

"So, you know he talks about affirmations and thinkin positive, blahzay blahzay?

"Right."

"I finally get why *the powers that be* love Hip-Hop so much."

"Why?"

"It's the opposite of positive affirmations. They claim you can rewire your brain to shift from negative to positive thoughts, and the more times you repeat positive shit, the more you believe it and make it come true. Imagine what da hell we listened to growing up.

"Smack a hoe," says D-Wood

"Shoot the club up," Larry finishes his sentence.

D-Wood impersonates Tu-Pac's voice

"I see death around the corner."

They both rap together in Tu-Pac's voice,

"Gotta stay high while I survive

In the city where the skinny niggaz die

If they bury me, bury me as a G nigga,

No need to worry; I expect retaliation

In a hurry."

"Think about it; every hood across America was singing 'I see death around the corner.' Fear is instilled by spells. They usin our own words to put fear in us."

"That's why white people love hip-hop. We don't talk about killin them. We talk about killin us!"

They both crack up.

"Suppose a song says, 'Blacka blacka kill a cracka.' I bet they wouldn't put that song on no albums. As long as the picture we paint is us gettin murdered, nobody cares."

"Now it's all about Versace, you copied my style,"

They rap together,

"Five shots couldn't drop me. I took it and smiled."

"Who else took five shots and smiled?" said D-Wood.

"Who?"

"Yo, black ass, ain't it ironic you loved Fifty and Tupac, two rappers that got shot? Then, yo black ass got shot by the Police."

"What's our parent's favorite affirmation? 'You know you gon end up dead or in jail.' You got shot and went to prison. No wonder we used to call you four, you two for two haha."

D-Wood takes a hit of his joint. "That's why I had to get away from yo ass. Cuz guess who would have probably been with you when you got shot? Me! And you know ama die cuz I'm your light-skinned friend."

"And the light-skinned friend always dies. Ole Raheem in juice lookin ass."

Imitating Tu-Pac's voice, Larry says, "We run from the cops; we run from Radames, we run from security guards, we run from old man Quiles in a fucking bullshit's store when he comes at us with a bullshit gun. All we do is fuckin' run, feel like I'm on a goddamn track team." They both crack up.

"You have five minutes remaining on this call," said a voice.

"That's my cue. Ama holla back.

"Nigga it's been five years! Why you ain't out yet?"

"They keep bullshittin me. I still got open cases."

"You see why I stopped posting our songs or videos."

"Yeah, we should wait on that. How you been gettin bread?"

"I got a jizzob!" Larry finishes his sentence again

"Sum'm you might not nare know nuttin about," they both chuckle.

"A lotta folks ain't know I used to rap; they think I'm just some square-ass call center supervisor."

"You are a square-ass call center supervisor!"

"Fuck you," they chuckle,

"Aaaaaarrrgh,"

"What the hell was that?" says Larry.

"I don't know, but it was loud as hell."

"I gotta go anyway, holla back."

"One hunnid."

D-Wood hangs up as he hears more commotion coming from around the corner.

"Don't hurt em!" yells a woman.

Chapter Three

LADY, GET YOUR DOG!

D-Wood puts on a Kansas City Skully hat inside a studio apartment. With his cell phone in hand, he makes a recording of himself.

"Big black ass lips. If I stop smoking weed for ten years, will they turn back red?"

Eyes wide in a Kat Williams like voice, he starts recording a video on his phone.

"Wudup, Merica! IT'S STORYTIME! I know y'all see the craziness with the dog," he stops abruptly.

"Oh... you didn't see it? Cuz I'm horrible at holding up the camera. I gotta admit it, but no! This was trau-matizin; I never seen no dog eatin another one like this! And a white man on top ready to die for his dog like..." He leans back, mimicking a Caucasian man's voice, screaming, "Lady, get your dog!"

One hour earlier

"Aaaaaarrrgh,"

"What the hell was that?" says Larry.

"I don't know, but it was loud as hell."

"I gotta go anyway, holla back."

"One hunnid."

He gets out of his car and turns on his camera recorder.

"What the hell? These people are trippen over here," he says, walking towards the chaotic sounds. Turning the corner, he walks past a black woman keeping a safe distance from the mayhem.

"Oh my God," she screams.

"Aaaaarrrrrrrgh," a piercing yelp comes from one of the two dogs viciously fighting.

"Don't hurt the dog, don't hurt the dog!" exclaimed a black woman while two Hispanic construction workers swung two long polls unsuccessfully at the fighting dogs.

A Caucasian man is sprawled on the ground, trying to pull a Pitbull off his Mutt.

"Get your dog on a fuckin leash!" yells the white man furiously.

"He is on a goddamn leash!" A black woman rages back.

"Aaaaarrrrgh," a blood-curdling tormented scream of pain comes from the Mutt as the Pit Bull bites into him.

"Get your fuckin dog!" the white man wailed.

Bewildered, D-Wood places his backpack on the sidewalk

"I don't even know what to do," he mutters.

"I can't record this; I gotta help," he thinks as his phone records but aimed towards the ground.

Recording a Tik-Tok in a studio apartment. D-Wood narrates the incident while holding the mobile phone camera and recording himself.

"He was ready to die for his dog." He said while cheesing and revealing his dark gums.

"Aye, white people and y'all love dogs. That shit is precious. I love y'all; y'all so precious. He was ready to DIE! I could not think about holding the camera right on his ass."

He continues narrating;

"The black lady starts swinging at the man and his dog.

"This bitch is crazy!" thinks D.

"Don't you fuckin hit my dog!" yells the white man.

D tries to help grab one of the dogs with one hand and his phone in the other.

"You grab your dog, and you grab your dog," he shouted.

"The lady must have been on some extra gangster stuff ~ ion know what was going on with her - but maybe she just watched Bad Boys 3, you know what I'm sayin? She was like, 'we ride togetha, we die togetha!' Cuz she was trying to swing on the man like, *Uh* "he fake swings" Instead of grabbing her dog. Why wouldn't you grab your dog? That's your dog, but she wouldn't grab no dog. She just kept walking away! Then she started talkin about how she had lupus, which I won't make fun of. But I what I will make fun of, is why was you trying to jump these people with your dog!?"

"She won't grab her fuckin dog!" screams the white man.

"I'm getting the fucking leash!" she replies but continues pacing back and forth. Then, the Mutt lets out another long, heart-felt, high-pitched scream of agony.

"AAAAAAAARRHH!"

D-Wood's eyes widen,

"Oh my God, he's gonna kill him!" he thinks

Tears streaming, the white man lets out one more high-pitched wail.

"Get a hold of your fucking dog, lady!" The struggle continued. "You fucking bitch!" he screeched.

"Don't you call me a bitch!" she barks back. "I have a heart condition! I have lupus!"

D-Wood, unsure of which dog to choose, asks, "Which one is your dog?"

The Pitbull releases its grip for a split second, and D-Wood immediately jumps between the man and the Mutt.

The Pit squares up in front of him.

"Please don't bite me." He prayed in his head.

The Pit tries to jump past him, feeling like slow motion,

he grabs it by the scruff.

"Oh my God, I got him!" he thinks.

D-Wood shouts, "Come get your fuckin dog, lady!" while holding the dog by the scruff.

"Just calm down so your dog can calm down," says a black woman witnessing the struggle."

As he pants, the dog's long tongue hangs out of its mouth, "He smiling?" thinks D-Wood looking at him.

Strugling to get a rope around the Pitbull's head. The lady starts talking as if her and D-Wood were in mid conversation.

"Like last night, a woman was screaming because her boyfriend was beating her up." D cuts her off, anticipating police arrival.

"Here, I gotta go," he pushes her dog towards her. "I need to ensure you got your dog, and it's secure."

"I ain't tryna get to know yo crazy ass," he thought as he focuses his attention on her oversized red rain-boots.

He casts a quick peek up at the sky.

He stares at her red rain boots thinking, "It's not a cloud in the sky or a puddle on the ground."

"Who dressed you? Kanye West?" he says, snickering.

"In conclusion, both of the dogs lived. I see you folks getting mad sayin, 'Why you gotta point out it's a Pitbull?'"

Pitbulls are just recognizable, I don't know all dogs. For example, I don't know what a Terrier is, but I do know what a Collier is, cuz of Lassi. Umm, a German Shephard cuz the cops always on ya ass with a German Shephard. I know that dog, but you don't know all dogs.

I know what the guy's dog looked like, but I don't what it is. So, all I can say is, 'Pitbull and dog'; ain't nobody tryna demonize the Pitbull, although they do have a reputation.

I get where you're coming from cuz when I watch the news, they always callin brown people thugs and stuff, and I'm like, 'well, you called him a thug, but called the white guy a man? I get it, I called one dog a Pit, and the other one a dog. Like they're different, and they're not different. But they did look a lil different when he was on his ass, AHHHHHH!"

Chapter Four
AM I GOING CRAZY?

Steam escapes through a crack in the door. Sitting on the bathtub floor, D-Wood stares intensely at the water droplets on the shower curtain. Each drop sat still until another drop fell into it, then glided down the wall.

He smirks.

"We're all droplets stuck in the same place until we help each other move forward," he thinks, staring at the water.

"The ocean is just a quadrillion droplets."

Eyes stinging, he shields his face with the bottom of the shower curtain.

"We could live without parents, but

HOW TO FIGHT A PIG

not without water. We drink it, bathe in it, wash our clothes, cook.

Our plant can't grow without it. Water is life; why aren't we thanking you?" he thought, wiping water from his eyes.

"They say to thank God, but we should be thanking you too." He looks up at the water. "So, thank you, thank you, THANK YOU!"

His pupils disappear as his forehead vibrates intensely.

Cosmic energy shot into his body like dopamine rounds from an Ak 47.

"What the-," his pupils returned like kids from recess.

Then a voice said,

"You're welcome."

Water dripped from the over steamed bathroom ceiling. Stunned, he sat there in disbelief.

"Ama goin crazy?" he thought.

NEED $
For WEED

Chapter Five

HAPPY FOUR-TWENTY

(Phoenix, AZ: April 20, 2018)

A tiny hyperactive Yorkshire Terrier clings to D-Woods legs as he sits on a couch. He serenades the dog in an off-key, high-pitched voice,

"Secret loooooovaaaas yeah, that's what we arrrre." The dog jumps up and down excitedly. "Mmmmhh mhhhhhh una uhhh the way we feel." He trails off humming, googly-eying, and petting the dog.

A athletic, brown-skinned man snaps at the dog while sporting a Nipsey Hussle shirt.

"Mimi, get yo ass upstairs!"

Nails scratching the floor the dog dashes up the stairs.

"I'm ready to go, and we ain't got *NO WEED*!" An agitated, thick, Caramel-colored woman eyeballs her man.

"Gas-light me again!" he snaps back.

"He better not take all day on these brakes either!" she says, walking out the side door.

D-Wood whispers to Kwame,

"You know what gas-lightin means?"

"Hell nah," he responds, chuckling.

A basketball thumps against a rock driveway after swishing through a malfunctioning hoop. D sucks his teeth.

"Flat ass ball," he mutters.

Kwame walks over to him,

"Me and dude gotta go get a part from the store."

"Ight," D-Wood replies and takes another shot.

"Briiick!" yells Kwame, *clank*; the ball collides with the rim and falls to the ground with a sad plop. Kwame gets in a car with another man, and they pull off.

D-Wood walks over to the flat ball and sits on it. He turns his body towards a tree so no one can see his face.

His mind starts racing,

"Man... fuck her! Got me over here feelin like a dead beat, and she ain't even want my help. Now I'm a sperm donor, NO! She is a sperm stealer! My son ain't like me cuz I don't like you. If you wanted a baby, you coulda just said that. Caught me slippin on

an ecstasy pill and took the dick. If a woman came to my house drunk, and I had sex with her, I'd be a rapist. You was sober as hell, I came to sell you some weed, and you let me go in raw.

If you even mentioned a condom, I would've snapped out of it, but that's my dumb-ass fault, 'Let me give you a massage face ass.' The only reason he don't love me like he loves you is he didn't get to live with me. Of course, he scared of me, I don't take no shit, I was raised not to take no shit, and I ain't gon take no shit! Now he gotta go his whole life thinkin I don't love him, cuz I don't love you, dat's some BULL SHIT! Shut up! SHUT UP! SHUT UP!

You think the same thoughts every damn day. Let it go. Forgive her; Forgive yourself. Forgive her; FORGIVE YOURSELF! NO THOUGHTS!"

He placed his hand on the tree like a doctor with a stethoscope.

"I send you my love and appreciation."

Like smoke entering the lungs, energy shifted from him to the tree.

Bzzzzt, his shoulders tense up as the tree returns the energy. A child-like grin comes over his face.

"Thank you, I needed that!" he says, admiring the tree.

His eyes roll to the back of his head, then close. His lips pucker up as a succulent kiss breaks the silence.

His shoulders sag as he unwinds. As he strives to transfer every ounce of air to the front of his stomach, a vein in his neck pulsates. A complete blackout occurs.

"Deee!" yells Kwame; D-Wood opens his eyes, startled. "Get yo *Last Dragon Bruce Leroy* - looking ass up so we can go!"

He checks his cell phone with fluttering eyes; it is 9:00 p.m.

"Goddamn, three hours?"

"We had to go back and forth to the store. We ain't have the right tool to get this rotor off. I don't even wanna go to the party no more," says Kwame.

"Me either," D replied as he got in the back seat. "I can't believe it's Four-Twenty, and we ain't smoke no trees."

"Right," says Kwame as his girlfriend hops in the driver's seat.

"We ain't using him no more! I wouldn't wait this long to get into Heaven!" says Tasha.

"Cuz you know you ain't gettin in," says Kwame as he shuts his door. D-Wood cackles in the back seat.

"Shut the fuck up!" yells Tasha.

Chapter Six

GOOD SAMARITAN AND BLACK DON'T MIX!

A goofy grin covers D-Wood's face as he drives up the 202-highway eastbound in Phoenix, AZ.

"Sa Sa Sober than a bitch Sa Sa Sober than a bitch Sa Sa Sober."

He approaches a two-car accident. One vehicle was dangerously close to the highway on the right, while the second faced the wrong direction on the left.

"They might be hurt," he thinks as he slows down while surveying the cars.

"Maybe I should stop and check," he thinks, looking in his rearview mirror for ambulances.

He pulls off on the exit. Dress in a grey cashmere sweater and stylish jeans; his Jordans hit the highway's concrete moving.

A black car is parked a few feet away with three Hispanics inside.

"Y'all, okay?"

The driver gives an affirmative nod. He keeps walking toward the other two vehicles.

After a couple of steps, he thinks,

"What if they hurt, and I'm walkin."

He starts running up the hill, adrenaline pumping through his veins. He approaches the first car facing the right direction and discovers a Latina sitting in the driver's seat, unsettled, with her face barely visible through the window's dark tint. He taps on her window.

"You, okay?"

She nods her head in affirmative but doesn't roll down the window.

A white guy stood outside his car, talking on his phone,

"You good? Want me to help you push your vehicle?"

"No, I'm all right," he replies and continues his phone conversation. D-Wood starts walking toward his car, certain that no one needs help.

At 11:59 pm, he turns on his camera phone and records himself revealing the car accidents behind him.

"I know it's Four-Twenty and all, but damn."

He takes a couple of steps.

"These people got in a wreck, and I thought I would have to help somebody, but everybody's good. I'm goin back to my car, and thank God it wasn't me. Happy Four-Twenty."

After a few steps, a blinding beam covers him from above.

"Ahhhh shit!"

D-Wood yelps, squinting, as he recognizes a police helicopter.

Feeling like a villain in the spotlight, he reaches for his Kryptonite.

At 12:06 am, he begins video recording himself as the helicopter hovers above him.

"Wooow, now they're saying that I did something."

Like the circus's main attraction, the spotlight follows him.

"I stopped to help these people, and now they think I'm part of the shit. This is why black people should never stop to help nobody cuz then they will be gettin your ass."

He keeps walking and comes up to the first three Hispanics he saw parked by their car.

"Glad they still here," he thinks.

"Y'all hear this? The police? Y'all know I just stopped to help y'all, right?"

The driver nods his head sheepishly.

"They look scareder than three illegals at a Trump rally. Oh yeah! Po po be doin them dirty too, they prolly just as scared as I am," he thinks.

He keeps walking while recording on his phone. Then, he notices a blue blur approaching the corner of his eye. It's a Police officer running towards him.

"Me?" says D-Wood.

The officer sprints toward him, expressionless, like Bobby Bushay in *The Water Boy.*

"Are you serious?" he says.

Boom! The officer slams into him, and D-Wood lets his body go limp like Lebron James in the *Play-offs.*

"What'd I do?" he yells, falling to the ground.

The camera phone falls divinely to capture the Phoenix PD officer placing handcuffs on him.

"I literally came to a stop and helped these people; come on now!" he says, feeling like conquered cattle.

A DPS officer watches the Phoenix PD officer cuff him.

In a high-pitched, surprisingly calm voice, he says,

"Are you serious right now?" The officer offers no response.

After a minute, the officer speaks, "What car are you driving?"

"That one over there," he points towards his Chevy Impala ten feet away. "Do you see anything wrong with my car?"

The officer ignores his questions and talks to fellow officers.

"They fuckin my favorite sweater up," he thinks as cars slowly drive by, looking at him.

"Go down and ask the folks in the car accident if I approached them and asked if they needed help."

"We got word that someone was walking away from these accidents. Do you understand the misunderstanding?"

"I saw the helicopter over me, but they didn't say nothin."

His neck begins to ache.

"Why do I have to be in cuffs?"

"Because you were walking away," the officer replies.

"Wha wha what am I supposed to be doing on the side of the highway?" The officer notices D-Wood's phone on the ground recording. He picks it up, stops the recording, and takes it away.

"Can I have my phone back, please?"

The officer ignores him.

Like roadkill, he lay on the highway for twenty to thirty minutes listening to their small talk.

A supervisor officer arrives, after a short conversation, he says, "Let him go."

They pick up D-Wood and uncuff him. Immediately, he begins wiping dirt off his sweater.

"Can I get my phone back?" he asks furiously. The officer gets on his radio, "Does anyone have this guy's phone?"

A response says, "No, we don't have it."

On the roof of his car, D-Wood spots his phone.

"Can I get your badge number?"

"You want a badge number or you going home?" the officer replies. D-Wood shakes his head.

"Assholes!" He turns around, gets in his car, and drives off.

"Loosen up ya eyebrows," thinks D, catching his angry reflection in the rearview mirror.

"Got me lookin like Ice Cube," he smirks again. *"They done turned me into a Nigga with an Attitude,"* he chuckles.

He picks up his phone, goes to YouTube, and types *NWA.*

'F the police' pops up, and he clicks it.

"Fuck fuck fuck the police," blasts through his speakers as he bobs his head and pulls into a parking spot in an apartment.

His hairy knuckles grip the steering wheel, and his brows furrow again.

"I can't believe I let his weak ass knock me to the ground; I should have put a 'jook move' on his stupid ass.

Nah, then I'd be the next dead nigga on the news. Talkin bout, 'Can I see the misunderstanding?' They killin somebody every day over a misunderstanding! If I punched him in the damn face, it would be a misunderstanding that would get me locked up or killed. If it was a misunderstandin, why you ain't apologize?

I wonder how often a judge hears, 'it was a misunderstanding,' right before they lock somebody up. How the hell you gone knock someone to the ground without saying one word? How is that not assault?!" He wondered.

Chapter Seven

PLEASE, LET HIM GET AWAY!

His knuckles unclench the steering wheel as he leans back in the driver's seat.

"At least they didn't beat me this time."

His tongue slowly rubs over a lump inside his lip, triggering an old memory.

Two AM on the car stereo. Grand Daddy Purple marijuana filled the vehicle. In unison, D-Wood and Larry bob their heads as they rhyme back and forth in freestyle to a hip-hop instrumental.

D-Wood starts to rap; "I ain't like rap for a minute man but I can still bust one quicker than a minute man."

Larry Wayne continues the rap; "No limit man, like P Mommy sayin that she squirts But it's lookin like Pee, hahaha."

D-Wood raps on; "All on my white T And this ain't the first time She done messed up like three."

Larry Wayne continues; "Ain't anotha nigga like me So, every time she talks She uses words like we."

D-Wood continues; "But the bitch ugly That'll be the truth.

If I showed you a picture That'll be the proof, ha-haha."

D-Wood raises his phone and shows a picture of a girl in his messenger. They both burst out cackling like hyenas.

Larry stops smiling, his eyes close to a squint, "We gettin jacked!"

He exits the driver's side door and takes off like he was handed a baton.

"Fuuck!" D-Wood roars jumping out of the car. He purposefully slams the door to attract attention. He dashes toward a cement wall that leads to a neighborhood.

An officer yells,

"You think you're gonna make it over that wall?"

Sprinting towards the wall, he jumps as hard as he can. A taser flies past him as he clears the wall. The officer doesn't attempt to give chase.

He scans the backyard as his feet hit the ground.

"Think," he says to himself as he walks around in a circle. Right next to a pitch-black house, he spots a fence he could easily scale.

"I don't feel like running from the cops all night; I didn't even do nothin!" he thinks.

"I hope that fool got away, and this wasn't for nothin." He can hear the cops on the other side of the wall.

"They're gonna take my car if I don't go back," he mutters.

He yells out,

" Didn't know it was the cops. I'll come back over the wall only by the street where people can see me."

A cop responds,

"Okay, come on."

He gets to the wall close to the street and jumps up, leaning on the wall with his upper body.

As the cops reach up for him, he remembers he has weed in his pocket.

"Whoa," he pretends to lose his balance and falls back to the ground. He pulls the weed out and tucks it behind a tree growing up against the wall. He jumps back up and begins to cross the wall in the direction of two Glendale police officers. As soon as his leg went over the wall, *'Bink, Bink,'* they started beating him with their Batons.

'Bink. Bink. Bink. Bink,'

"Stop resisting! Stop Resisting!"

"They know damn well I'm not resisting," thinks D as he lies on the ground catching blows.

'Bink. Bink. Bink. Bink.'

Adrenaline flowed through him.

"I thought this would hurt a lot more," he thinks, putting his hands behind his back.

'Bink. Bink. Bink.'

"I swear I could get up and whoop both of these weak ass bastards."

They cuff him and put him in the trunk of the police car.

Eyes closed, rocking back and forth, he prayed.

"Please let him get away. Please let him get away."

Five minutes pass. He smiles as the police car starts.

"That lucky bastard must've got away. Good shit!"

A bewildered look comes over his face.

"Ain't this a bitch." he thinks, tilting his head.

"My dad's belt hurt worse than the damn police batons. Man, ain't no way in hell I woulda been able to put my hands behind my back if I ain't get them ass whoopin as a child.

An annoyed look covers his face.

Wooow, he knew I was gon get beat like a slave one day, so he beat me to prepare me for it. That's some certified bull shit!" He smirks at the thought.

"That was like a deep tissue massage compared to that belt on my naked ass." He sucks his teeth, *"That's so annoying. I ain't even mad at ya, Pops. You definitely prepared me for that."*

He licks his upper lip,

"Salty", he thinks, tasting blood.

A side mirror reflection exposed a chunk of meat hanging stuck in his teeth.

Chomp. Chomp. Clamping his teeth together causes the police officer to turn around.

"We got ourselves a biter."

D-Wood's underbite prevented his front teeth from touching closely enough to bite through the skin, so he had to leave it hanging.

Rubbing the inside of his lip with his tongue, D-Wood adjusts his driver's seat to lie back.

His face lights up as he picks up his cell phone and goes to his videos.

"I was recording when that asshole tackled me." He says to himself loudly.

He logs into Facebook and starts typing a post,

'*A brotha can't even stop to check on an accident without being attacked by the police.*'

After posting two videos, he finally leans back in the driver's seat and closes his eyes.

Chapter Eight

YOU DON'T STOP TO HELP NOBODY!

Bzzt Bzzzzzzzzt, D-Wood's phone vibrates beside him. He picks up his buzzing cell phone with his eyes still closed and answers while wiping eye boogers from his eye.

"Yooo"

"What the hell happened to you last night?" says Kwame laughing uncontrollably.

"You got arrested? How the hell that happen? I just saw the video!" He starts cracking up again. D-Wood joins him as they both laugh hysterically.

"Wassa name said you went to jail last night, and I thought he had to be trippen, then I saw the video and was like, what in the entire hell is going on here?" Kwame asks, finally controlling his laughter.

"Man," replies D.

"That video is *soooo* damn funny! The way you fell and was holding the camera catching your face as you fell had me soooo weak! Oh my God, D, what the hell was you thinkin stoppin to help some people? You don't stop to help nobody! You know you black!"

"Bruh," says D.

"I bet you won't stop to help nobody else. Black ass always trying to be nice, hahahaha."

"Black people can't do nothin', hahaha," says D-Wood cracking up again.

D can also hear Kwame's girlfriend, Tasha, giggling in the background.

Kwame says,

"They didn't know you was a videographer; how did you get the cop's face in it too?"

"It's crazy, right? The phone fell in the perfect position to catch the cop's face," replies D.

"I don't ever stop to help nobody because of shit like that. Damn! That video is doing numbers right now."

"For real? You called before I got to see any reactions to it."

"Next time you see an accident, keep ya black ass in the car. Leave that to the white people!"

"Shut up nigga. I'm helpin!" They both crack up again.

"Real talk; I'm glad you're good, though. That's crazy as hell! Hit me back later."

"Most def, one hunnid," replies D.

They hang up, and then he checks his Facebook.

"He was not lying," says D-Wood looking at his phone. The video had only been up for nine hours, and it already got Six =-hundred-plus notifications, three hundred-plus comments, one hundred and fifty plus shares, twelve thousand plus views.

"Damn... out of all the videos I post, this is what people wanna see? Me getting knocked to the ground by a cop," He thinks.

He reads through some of the comments:

"Sue their asses!"

"Glad you're okay."

"That's racial profiling."

"Lawsuit."

"This has to stop! "

"Sue their asses!"

Chapter Nine

NO CAMERAS BY THE CAT FOOD

Clank, clank. D-Wood kicks the side of his grocery cart, avoiding a wall of canned goods.

"*Hot sauce,*" he thinks as an elderly lady flees the aisle he is about to enter.

"Mmmh," an unwelcoming sensation halts him in his tracks.

"I ain't walkin in that," he thinks, backing up his grocery cart to avoid walking in the lady's aura.

"I get the worst carts," he thinks, smiling at a raw salad in his basket.

" I send my love and appreciation to you, broccoli, spinach, raisins, pineapple, and cauliflower. Thank you all for your wonderful energy." He hovers his hand over the salad. Energy flows from him to the veggies, his shoulders tighten, and his forehead vibrates.

He continues pushing his grocery cart up the aisle and pulls into the Cat food aisle, looking up.

"No cameras by the Cat food aisle," he says, wiping the cart handle with the bacteria wipe.

He reaches down, grabs a handful of salad, and stuffs it in his mouth. His mouth tenses up around the food as if it were scorching hot. Then, a toothy grin comes over his face.

"Thank you," he grabs a big box of Cat food and tosses it in his cart. The aroma from the chicken wings grab his attention,

"I send my love and appreciation to you, beautiful chicken."

Again, his shoulders tense up, and his forehead vibrates. Then, he smiles and continues, "I hope you are enjoying your next..." he pauses, unsure what to say. "Existence. I can't wait to become one with you." He finishes.

Bzzzt, vibrate,

"We are already one," says a voice.

Glancing up, he notices a short Mexican security guard walking up the aisle toward him. He grabs a pack of tortillas and covers his food with it. The man stares at his cart as he passes by.

At that moment, his phone rings; it is from an unknown number. D-Wood answers, " Hello."

"Hi, I'm Val with Grover's Law firm. Is this David?" A woman's voice responds. "This is him."

"Hi, I received your email, including your video. I'm sorry that happened to you."

"Do you think I have a case?" he replies.

"I can't say for sure. Do you have any damages?"

"My arm is a little sore still."

"Did you go to the hospital?"

"Yeah," he replies.

"I went and got X-Rays on my arm, but they said it was pretty much okay."

"I don't think we can do much for you, but if you want us to try, you can retain us for three hundred.

"Three hundred ...? well, I'll call you back and let you know whether or not to proceed."

He hangs up and starts pushing his cart toward the front register. He tries to throw away his empty box of chicken wings, but the hole in the trash can is too small. Trying not to draw any attention, he forces the square box through the hole.

"Yuck," he groans, pulling his hand out with some unidentified sticky substance on his finger.

He gets to the register and scans his salad,

"*Forgot my drink,*" he realizes.

A mature Asian employee stood by,

"Ma'am, can you void this? I forgot something."

She looks at his half-eaten salad and looks back at him. She makes an eating gesture with her hand while pointing at the salad.

"*Oh shit, she knows I ate the salad,*" thinks D. She keeps shaking her head and pointing to the salad. D-Wood smiles and pretends not to understand, re- alizing she must be deaf. She reaches into her pocket, and takes out a pen and pad. She writes something, and shows him the note.

'*You're not supposed to eat,*' it reads.

D-Wood motions; she gives him the pen and paper. He writes on the paper and hands it back. She smiles as she reads his response. D-Wood looks at her and starts licking his fingers and smacking his lips like he is eating something delicious.

She points at him and then to the door, giving him an embarrassed smile.

His expression immediately changes as he turns around. A burning horse-radish flavor took over his mouth. He coughs as he recalls sticking his fingers in the garbage. "Tastes like fake ass wasabi," he mut- ters. "Aaarrrggghhh!"

Chapter Ten

THE 1983 LAWSUIT

*T*ap, *tap.* Tiny flowers fall onto the hood of D-Wood's parked impala. With the driver's seat reclined, he skimmed through YouTube comments from the video he posted.

"Sue the bastards!"

"This is why I don't stop to help."

"Nothing will happen to the cops."

"They do this all the time."

"Can't believe this happened after you stopped to help."

Then he saw one that he hadn't seen before. It read;

"You should file a 1983 Excessive Force Lawsuit."

"What's that even mean?" he asked himself as he searched it on Google. When he found it on oogle, it read; *"Section 1983 refers to a federal statute that allows people to sue for certain kinds of civil rights violations, including excessive police force."*

　　　　　　　　　HOW TO FIGHT A PIG

"How come I never heard these words? " he muttered to himself. He glanced up at the wall of shrubs and asked, "Bush, what do you think? Should I file a 1983 Lawsuit?"

Bzzzz vibrates,

"*Duh,*" says the Bush

"Hahaha, really, Bush? 'Duh', that's what you have to say? So, you think I can win?"

Bzzz vibrates.

"Of course, you can win; how could you lose?" the Bush replies.

"*Bush is right; I didn't do anything wrong,*" he thinks.

Bzzzz vibrates,

"I'm not a Bush!"

"Haha, Obviously, you are more than a Bush, but I have no idea what you are. Do you have a name?" No response.

"I don't know what else to call you but Bush, my bad."

Bzzz vibrates,

"I know."

"Thanks for the advice, Bush. Ama do it; I'm filing a lawsuit."

On YouTube, he types a response to the '1983 Excessive force' comment, "*Thanks for the info!*"

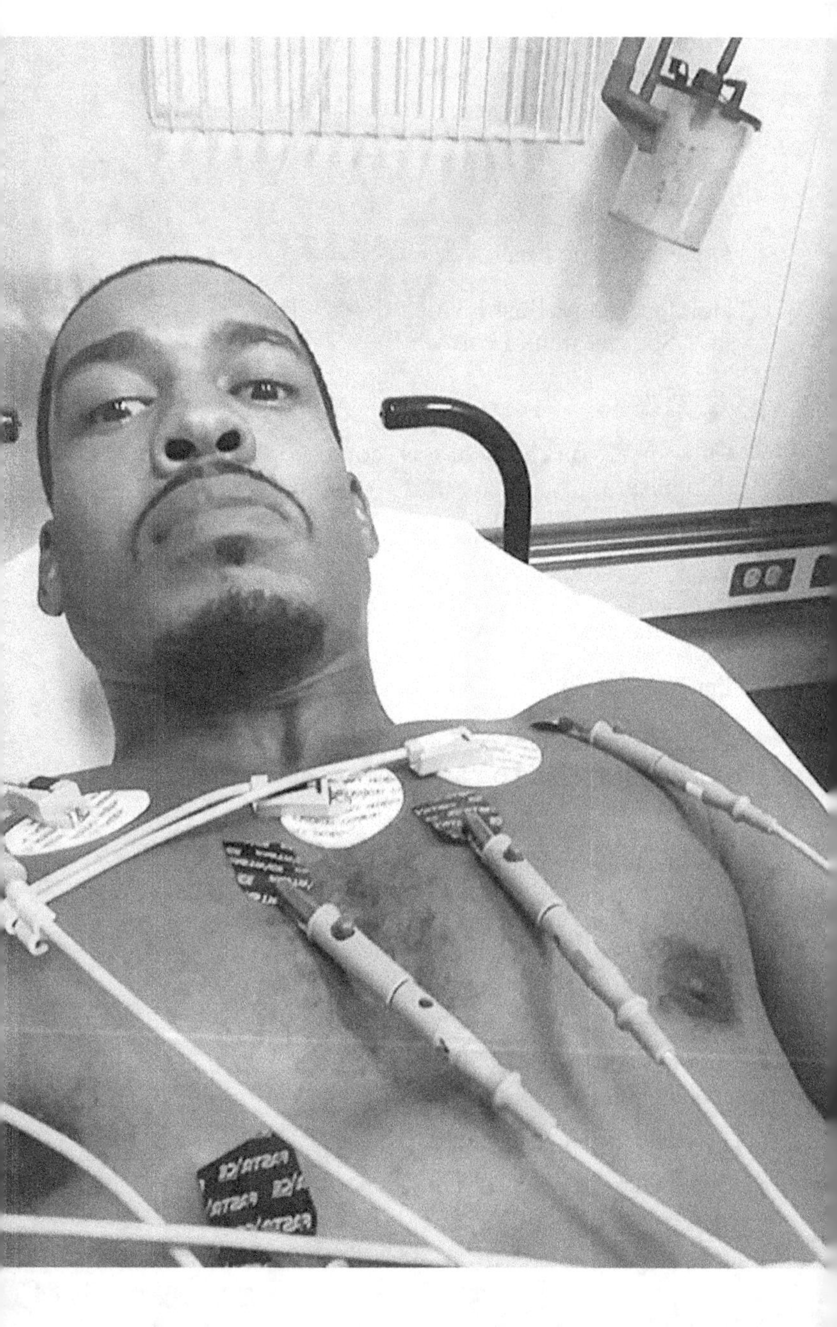

Chapter Eleven

THE DIAGNOSIS

A young dark-skinned flowered-dressed woman hands D-Wood a clipboard.

"Please fill out this questionnaire and return it to me." she says. He takes the clipboard back to his seat, and the lady walks by with his eyes following behind her.

"*Mmmmm, she could get it,*" he thinks.

He reads the questionnaire in his head.

"*Repeated, disturbing memories, thoughts, or images of a stressful experience from the past.*

1 Not at all

2 A little bit

3 Moderately

4 Quite a bit

5 Extremely."

He puts an X beside Quite a bit.

"Suddenly acting or feeling as if a stressful experience were happening again (as if you were reliving it)."

He puts an X beside Quite a bit.

"Feeling emotionally numb or unable to have loving feelings for those close to you."

He puts an X beside Quite a bit.

"Feeling as if your future will somehow be cut short."

He puts an X beside Quite a bit.

"Feeling irritable or having angry outbursts."

He puts an X beside Quite a bit.

"Hahaha," he laughs, thinking, *"The whole hood has PTSD."*

Fifteen minutes later, he sits across from a mature blond Caucasian woman wearing an emerald green silk blouse. He discreetly scans the room and notices the numerous psychology degrees covering the wall.

Holding back his tears, D-Wood speaks in a low, monotone voice.

"I was knocked down by the police a few weeks ago. In the HOV lane, a police vehicle approached me from behind. I was certain that I wasn't driving too fast. They signaled me to pull to the side. So, I change lanes... what the... " he hits himself under his arm.

"Is that a bug?" he thinks. He reaches under his shirt and feels a bead of sweat dripping from his armpits.

"*This natural shit ain't workin, I need some de-odorant,*" he thinks.

"You, okay?" says the psychiatrist.

"Yeah, I'm startin to sweat just thinkin about it," she scribbles in her notepad. "I thought it was a bug under my shirt, but it's sweat. Sorry, that kinda sounds gross," he chuckles.

She smiles. "I'm no stranger to sweat. I wear men's deodorant because women's don't cut it for me."

"But you're still a woman, right?"

She wrinkles her brow.

"Yes, yes."

"Hey, sorry I had to ask. Hashtag *Trans-Therapist* could be blowin up right now, haha." Her eyes widened.

"My bad. Ama focus," says D-Wood.

No longer sounding sad, he continues.

"So, police cars drove by without even glancing at me, and I couldn't breathe. Then I noticed my feet started to feel numb. I could barely push the pedals, but I knew I was near the Hospital, so I managed to drive there as my feet and breathing worsened. I made it to the ER feeling like I was about to die."

"What did the doctors say at the ER?" asks the psychiatrist.

"The doctors diagnosed me with a panic attack. So, they gave me an EKG (electrocardiogram) and injected somethin in my butt. The doctor recommended I see a therapist if I experience these feelings again, so here I am."

"Thank you, David. Just give me one moment."

She scribbles on a piece of paper.

"She got a lil Betty-White thing goin on. She might get it after a bottle of Jack," he thinks.

She stops writing,

"After hearing what you say and reviewing your questionnaire, I recommend you come back for counseling every twelve weeks. I believe you have an unspecified anxiety disorder, an unspecified depressive disorder, Anxious Distress Specifier, Panic Disorder and Post-traumatic stress disorder."

D-Wood stares back at her with a blank face. He examines her physique as she stands up, thinking, *"She kinda thick."*

"I suggest you take a break from watching the media. It can't help but add to your anxiety with everything going on. I'm going to prescribe a few medications, and I hope to see you soon."

His expression hardens at the sound of medication.

Four years earlier

A dim light bounces perfectly off a stunning dark Ethiopian woman's skin. Next to her sits D-Wood, pretending not to feel her death stare. Instead, he continues watching a *Stars* episode of *"Power."*

On the television, a Hispanic woman pushes a black man named Ghost onto a bed and passionately kisses him.

Shaking her head and staring at D-Wood, she says,

"You niggaz love you some Mexicans, don't ya?"

"I thought you ain't use the *N-word*."

"I ain't until I got with one," she says without batting an eye.

"You darker than me soundin like a white supremacist." Mimicking her, he continues, "'You Niggaz love you some Mexicans' News flash, Angela is not Mexican; she's Puerto Rican," he says, turning to her with a smirk.

Suddenly, as if a light bulb went off in his head, he says, "Hold up. Nigga YOU used to date a Mexican dude back in Washington! Or should I say Jajajajajaja hahahaha. No nigga, I don't love Mexicans; WE love Mexicans!" He cracks himself up.

"Don't try to change the subject. I ain't cheat on you with no Mexican. YOU CHEATED ON ME WITH A MEXICAN!"

"See, dis is why I didn't wanna watch this fuckin show cuz I knew you was gon act like this!"

"Oh, so you already seen this show?"

"Hell, yeah! But ama kill myself if I have to watch one more episode of Basketball Wives!"

"You don't like basketball wives?"

"It's better than watchin a child come out a vagina."

"You said vagina?... awwwww baby; I'm rubbing off on you. You usually say 'Pussy'. Aww." She smiles, amused.

He holds back a smile,

"SHUT UP!"

She digs inside her purse and pulls out a pill bottle.

"Wanna Percocet? It's a thirrrrrty?"

He looks at the pill skeptically, "Am I going to be slumped over the toilet like yo ass the other night?"

"I wasn't sleep on no toilet!"

"The other day, you was literally slumped over, *sleeping* on the toilet!"

"Whatever!"

"If I take the pill, you gon shut up and watch the show?"

"Yeah," He takes the pill from her, throws it in his mouth, and swallows it.

Bzzzz, his cell phone vibrates, and he receives a text message.

"*Wanna smoke a blunt?*"

Twenty minutes later

A Hispanic woman sits in the driver's seat. D-Wood sits in the passenger seat, admiring the blunt she passed him.

"You ain't roll this," he says skeptically.

"It didn't roll itself," she says proudly.

"Okay, go on with ya bad self. I woulda never guessed you smoked weed."

"Well, I don't advertise it. I try to keep it *professional* at the job."

"I couldn't hide it if I wanted to; my black ass lips give me away errtime."

"Bahahaha," she cracks up. "They ain't that black."

"The hell they ain't. My lips used to be pink like Shemar Moore from *Criminal minds.* Then I started smokin these damn blunts, and one day, I woke up with Wesley Snipes' lips. I been thinkin bout suing *Swisher Sweet* for years. My lips are the same color as my knees now!

"Hahahaha," she cracks up again. "So, what were you doing?"

"Watchin Power..." he suddenly stops talking,

"Zzzzzzzzzzz," he instantly began snoring.

Her eyes squint, confused.

"Am I dreaming?" he thinks, eyes still closed,

"Zzzzzzz," faintly, he hears snoring.

"Is that me?" he thinks.

His Head tilted to the side, and he opens his eyes,

"Was I snoring?" he asks.

"Uh, yeah," she replies, sounding annoyed.

"I could hear myself. I ain't never fell asleep talkin like that before. I feel like I fell asleep in the middle of a sentence."

"You did fall asleep in the middle of a sentence."

"Zzzzzzzz," he is snoring again.

Concerned, she yells, "DAVEED!"

Sitting in the driver's seat of his car in a call center parking lot, D-Wood hits the speaker on his cell phone.

"You have a collect call from Larry Wayne at Arizona correctional facility. Press one to accept or press two to ignore."

"What it do, fam?"

"Hello"

"Hello? Why you sound like that? You ain't never answered the phone with 'Hello.'"

"I don't know; I just called out of work, and I'm sitten in this parkin lot tryin to figure out what the hell is wrong with me."

"Why you call out?"

"Nigga... this shit don't even feel right comin out of my mouth but... I feel sad as shit right now. Like I literally wanna cry."

"How? I'm in prison, but *you* wanna cry?"

"The weird part is I don't know why; I feel like I'm on my fuckin period."

"Check ya pussy, you bleedin?"

"Riiiight! That's how I really feel - like a whole bitch. Last night I was with this ... ooooooh shit! I know what's wrong with me!" He suddenly yells, like a light bulb just came on in his head.

"What?"

"Geneva gave me a Perc last night, and not a lil one either; it was a thirty! My stupid ass tried to go smoke a blunt with this chick, and I fell asleep mid-sentence talkin to the bitch."

"Hahahaha," they both crack up.

"She had to have her homegirl drive me home; it was that bad."

"Daaamn!"

"Yeah! And I been sitten at my desk for the last hour fightin back tears *nigga*. If this is what depression feels like, no wonder muphuckas be killin they self."

"Broooo, you know what? I ain't never told you this. But one time, I took a Vic, and the next day I was drivin. I had to stop the car because I broke down cryin, and I mean bawlin. Snot bubbles was comin out my nose." They both crack up again.

"You ain't never told me that shit; that's comedy." D-Wood says, amused."That's exactly what I wanted to do. I was just sitten in front of my computer at work feelin like I just found out I was gay. 'Why do I have these feelings?'" D-Wood replies in a sad voice.

"You're fuckin stupid!"

"Nigga I ain't had a lump in my throat since my dad came to the school and found out I was makin fake report cards. At least, I know why I was cryin. This Perc just activated the whole bitch in me."

"Bitch activated"

"Sensitivity activated!"

"Hoe ass nigga activated! hahahaha"

"How the S on your chest stands for sad?"

"Super soft ass nigga."

"This why so many people depressed, everybody on these damn pills!"

"Hell yeah, it's fuckin with the chemicals in our brains. I ain't even cry at my sentencing."

"Right. There ain't nothin wrong with cryin, we just don't do it. Prolly cuz we grew up hearin, 'I'll give you som'n to cry about!' So, if we ain't gettin our ass whooped, ain't no reason to cry."

"For real."

"We know how to deal with depression cuz our daddies ain't put up with that shit. 'You better fix ya mothaphuckin attitude, or you gon get ya ass whooped.'"

"We got punked out of depression, hahaha, 'I'll give you som'n to cry about!'"

"You know who be cryin? Abusive ass niggas."

"How you gon beat a chick up and then cry about it? haha"

(Sobbing voice) "I'm gon change, baby; I swear, no more dark liquor, hahaha."

"That was once me. You remember Angie?"

"Yeah,"

"To this day, I don't remember what she said to me while we was drinkin, but she said som'n super slick while we was sittin in her lil ass bed. Bro, I smacked a whole hand print in her face. I felt so bad the next day, and I cried like a lil bitch." In a sobbing voice he continues, "I don't wanna be like my Daddy!" They both crack up at that.

"That's when I knew my pimp's hand was not strong. You gotta have a cold ass heart to be beatin broads up cuz you can't control yaself. That's wack as fuck!"

"Hell yeah. You already know me and my baby got matchin bite marks. You bite me, ama bite ya ass back!" they both laugh.

"The funny thing is some women love depressed ass dudes. This guy Pete Davidson keeps gettin hoes and always cry about how depressed he is.»

"He gettin too much pussy, we ain't know ejaculatin too much causes depression and makes us stupid, but you niggaz ain't ready for that convo."

An operator's voice comes on the line.

"You have five minutes left on this call."

"Ama leave you with this; a relationship is like Milk: you gotta keep it cold if you want it to last longer." they both crack up.

"Ight. Ama jack off one last time, then kill myself."
They both hang up laughin.

As D-Wood enters his flat, he notices a yellow notepad on his glass coffee table.

"Thanks for making me feel like shit," Geneva says
as she walks in wearing a red robe.

"What are you talkin about? Why is my notebook
on the table?"

"Because I was reading it."

"You know I don't like anyone reading my shit," D
retorts, grabbing his notepad.

"So, you're my crutch?"

"What?"

"I read your song, and it said, 'I can't be your crutch
no more.' You think you're my fucking crutch?"

"Geneva, I write songs when I'm drunk. I don't
know what the hell you want me to say."

"You called me a crackhead!"

"I didn't call you no crackhead!" He opens his
notebook and finds the page.

"Okay, I called you a crackhead."

"I fucking hate you right now!"

Whispering to himself, he reads a few lines.

"I can't be ya crutch no moooore; If you can't walk,
it's time to crawl."

"I wrote this after you fell asleep on the fucking *TOILET* while listening to Jamaican music. Fuck it. Ama sing the shit." In a horrible Jamaican accent, he starts singing.

"I can't be ya crutch no mooooore

If you can't walk, it's time to craaaawl

I gotta let you hit rock bottom

Hit rock bottom

Hit rock bottooooom

I gotta let you hit rock bottom

Hit rock bottom

Hit rock bottooooom hey

How long you gon be doing this before you get a clue?

How many faces do you need to see turn blue?"

He stops,

"I seen you go to three funerals of people you personally knew that took the same pills as you."

He continues,

"How much money are you really gon spend

Tally up the whole year ya head really gooon spin"

He stops again,

"You got me over drafting my account every week, over fucking pills."

He continues,

"You got too many crack head tendencies

Chain smokin like a brudda with some Hennessy

Them Opiates will fuck with ya chemistry

The hustlin ass doctas gotta be a trillion-dollar in-
dustry.

I'd rather live dirty, see a mouse

than have you sniffen them pills to clean da house

And I hope it hurts when you hear dis

I hope and pray it turns you into something fearless

and you embrace those thoughts of depression.

Every thought is a blessin

you have another chance to learn a lesson, yeah

I know you heard about recovery on the blogs

dis won't be da first time you been sick as a dog

if you ain't hurtin you ain't gettin betta

Lifes a bitch you act like you ain't never met her

And as the days grow longa

embrace your opportunity to get stronga

This is one addiction

you have to give an eviction

All them damn prescriptions

gon have you fitten descriptions

But I can't be your crutch no moooore

If you can't walk, it's time to crawl"

Geneva stands, looking more embarrassed than angry.

"See, I didn't call you no crackhead; I said you have crackhead tendencies."

"That's the same fuckin thing, David!"

He grabs the sides of her robe and brings her closer.

"Okay, maybe I did call you a crack head in the second verse. But that only means I'm in love with a crackhead."

She smiles as a tear drops down her eyes.

"You remember Def Comedy Jam, 'Walked in my home, all my shit was gone, I'm in love with a crackhead,'" he chuckles.

"It's not funny, David!" She hits him as he grabs her and brings her close. "It's actually a good song, but your accent sucks, boo!"

"I know."

"How did you read that so well? I couldn't understand half the stuff you wrote."

"That's why I don't like people reading it! I leave out words when I write, but I still see them when I read it. So, stay out of my shit! I also write about bitches and hoes in here, which I'm sure you don't wanna read, so leave my notebooks alone!"

"Shut up."

He snaps back to reality in the psychiatrist's office.

"I don't want to be on medications, to be honest."

"How about we just try it for a month, and we'll see how it makes you feel." says the woman.

"I guess." He replies.

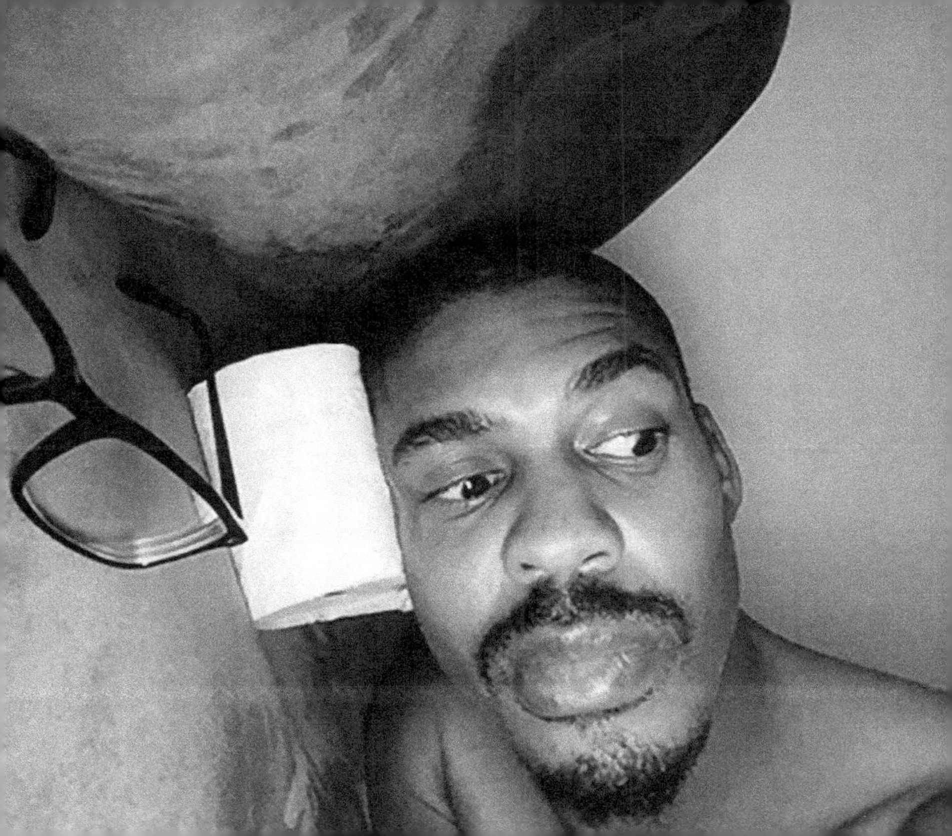

Chapter Twelve
THE PILL POPPER

The flagrant scent of cinnamon filled the room, covering the ripe smell of funk creeping from the closet. D-Wood sits on a couch alone on the second floor of his cousin's studio apartment with one King-sized bed, a flat-screen TV, a sofa, and a kitchen all in one room. *Criminal Minds* plays on the flat screen.

D-Wood walks out of an opened patio door and picks up a huge glass jar of water sitting in the sun. Next to it is a quartz crystal.

"Soaking up the sun, my guy?" he says to the crystal.

After taking a pill, he starts vigorously spinning the big glass jar of water until a twister vortex forms inside. His forehead vibrates as he stares at the vortex.

"*Why does that happen when I do that?*" he thinks.

"I send my love and appreciation to this water." His eyes shut tight as his energy flows to the water, and he then takes a swig.

Bzzzt vibrates; he smiles at the water,

~  ~

Twenty minutes later

D-Wood picks up a pharmacy bag and flips it, spilling three pill bottles across the sofa.

"These pills got me feelin like I did a line," he thinks, picking up two bottles.

Sitting on the couch while holding a pill bottle in each hand, he shakes the right one, *chicka.* Then he shakes both pill bottles, *chicka, chicka.*

"That's crazy! These pills sound like Maracas," he thinks.

Chicka, chicka, the pills in the bottle went as he shook it. Imitating Elvis Presley, he starts singing and dancing with the pills.

"Pill popper do the pill popper (chicka, chicka)

Pill popper doin the pill popper (chicka, chicka)

Pill poppin, doin the pill popper,

She was ass Poppin, and doin that ass proper. Ooooooooh they love when they hear that sound (chicka, chicka)

That sound there means it's going doooown (chicka, chicka)

Right down, down, down, down ya throat

Life is rough and I just can't cope

Got these pills cuz I'm depressed

They said take these pills, and you'll feel ya best

I took these pills and I got dressed

Then I met me a girl and we had sex

Doin the pill popper, do the pill popper (chicka, chicka)

Pill popper, do the pill popper (chicka, chicka)

Pill Popper, doin the pill popper

She was ass Poppin and doin that ass Proper

Ooooooh those pills had me feeling groovy

I felt so good I almost ate the booty

I said, go ahead, bend over Judy

She said, not now, boy I really have to dooty

Then she wiped her butt with a pair of wipes

I wonder if that saves my tongue from a parasite

I posted a pic, it only got a pair of likes

Took a couple more pills and went back to paradise

Now we pill poppin doin the pill popper (chicka, chicka)

Pill Poppin, doin the pill popper (chicka, chicka)

Pill Poppin, doin the pill popper

She was ass Poppin and doin that ass proper

Everybody put ya glasses up to toast

Today I got the doctor to up my dose

Went from five up to fifteen grams

And started dancing like Elvis to the old-school jam

Say that line for the white folks

Crushed the pills up in a line just like coke yay

Somebody shoulda told ya boy

Remember when Cat Stacks told on Soldier boy

And said he

Sniffed one line

Sniffed two lines

Sniffed threeeeeeee lines

(Hahaha)

Pill Poppin, do the pill popper (chicka, chicka)

Pill Poppin, doin the pill popper (chicka, chicka)

Pill Poppin doin the pill popper

She was ass Poppin and doin that ass Proper."

He finishes the lines and breaks out into fits of laughter.

Ain't
easy!

Chapter Thirteen

STEP ONE

D-Wood walks through a metal detector, downtown. He follows an arrow pointing to Phoenix Law Library. Finally, he walks through the door wiping sweat from his forehead. A young light-skinned girl walks up to him, and asked politely,

"Are you looking for family court documents?"

"No." He replied.

"Thank you Jesus," she said, smiling .

"I need to find out how to file a complaint."

"Complaint against who?"

"The Phoenix Police Department."

"You don't have a lawyer?" she asks. .

"Nope."

"You can get instructions on how to file a complaint by buying a civil complaint form and instructions packet. You can find it on the computer over there and print it out."

"Thank you."

D-Wood finds the form complaint packet on the computer,

"Fuckin seventeen pages to print! Are there scriptures in this mothaphucker?"

A female employee looks in his direction. He continues reading out loud in a whisper.

"I am the person - *plaintiff* - that brings a complaint to the court to sue a person or entity - *defendant* - that I believe has done me wrong."

He starts feeling good about the whole thing.

"I am filing a civil complaint because I have civil rights," he smiles, thinking, *"Our ancestors died for these civil rights, and I'm about to fight for mine without getting my hands bloody. That's how you fight a Pig."*

He stops smiling as he continues to read the packet.

"Step one; I would have to name all of the defendants... mothabastard!"

His mind goes back to being on the highway, saying to an officer,

"Can I get your name and badge number?"

"Do you want our names, or do you want to go home?"

   HOW TO FIGHT A PIG

Eight hours later

"We are closing in 5 minutes," says one of the female staff. He exhales a long sigh realizing he's still on step one.

   "What did I get myself into?" he mutters as he unplugs his USB drive.

Chapter Fourteen
THE RESPONSE

A waitress sets a couple of beers down at a table with two Caucasian women.

"It's Karaoke night on the other side and open mic night on this side," the waitress informs the women.

"Well, neither of us can sing, so we'll stay here," one of the women replies.

The other woman observes the empty chairs and responds, "We'll be the audience."

Holding the microphone, D-Wood speaks to the almost empty bar.

"Oh, my God! We have two audience members. Give them a round of applause, guys."

A table full of comics applauds the two ladies.

"You guys together? Married?"

"She just got divorced," says one of the ladies.

"Congrats, I love divorced women. Divorced women do everything a good wife used to do; shut up, put out, and shave that bush down there." He says and looks at his private parts.

"Hahaha," the lady's friend spits her beer out.

"She finally shaved!" exclaims her friend laughing.

"I used to hate Bush, not a hairy vagina, but the President someone through a shoe at. I hated him less when I saw his dodge game; that was impressive. So, why did you boycott cutting your grass?"

"Haha, he cheated," says a lady.

"Oh damn. Well, did you have any evidence?"

"He admitted it."

"Oh wow, it couldn't be me; I ain't admittin nothin. I got accused of cheatin, but this girl ain't have no evidence. I treated her the same way the cops treated me when I submitted a complaint about one of their officers. Their lawyer always responded the same way to every accusation, no matter how much evidence I presented.

"I figured if it works for the courts, why not for me? So, when she sent me a text sayin, 'I know you were with that bitch last night.' You wanna know what I said?" He takes out a piece of paper.

"Let's hear it, says a lady."

"Defendant is without sufficient information to form a belief as to the truth or falsity of the allegations."

"And how'd that work out for ya?" says a lady.

"She blocked me."

Chapter Fifteen
CAUGHT SLIPPIN'

Eyes closed, water bounces off D-Woods head in the shower. He holds his hand out and clicks his fingers together like he's at an open mic for Poetry.

"People are who they are
they gon be who they be
you can't see what they see

cuz you ain't seen what they seen
from a mom that's a fiend
she plots and she schemes
she can't stop the dreams
so she stops and she screams;
'you lil bad muphucka
you the only thing I wish I never had muphucka'
and a lil boy cries uncontrollably
the look in his eyes says no consolin me
moms put a hole in me
and Pops ain't where he 'posed to be
and Grandma holds a rosery
and prays to the Lord
for the things she can't afford
for a daughter she adores
MI AMOR!
You cannot BE A WHORE!
I know it rains and it pours
and dealin with pain is a chore
but opportunity knocks
like a bang at the door
and with these words
she throws her cane to the floor;
'until you get stable, I will not enable
and you touch my grandson again
you gettin strangled!'"

His mind races as he dips his head under the shower. "She *wanted my baby but didn't want me in his life? That shit is crazy to me.*" He sits on the shower floor and lies back, shielding his eyes from the water.

"*If she didn't want me on the birth certificate, then she didn't want me in his life. She don't even know me! I gotta let this go. Even my Pops said kids are 'posed to be with they Mommas, except they suck at discipline! Why wouldn't you want his father around to help with that? It's so stupid.*

Is it just so you can have control? Now you got a lil boy runnin your house tellin you what to do, and all you can do is yell and be mad, and cryin to his grandparents sayin, 'he doesn't listen to me.' Of course, he don't listen to you, you soft as baby shit; he used to suck ya titty! He knows you won't hurt him. Y'all think love is babying, but love is also goin upside ya head. You prolly think I'm gonna beat the boy cuz I got beat, but I ain't gotta beat him; he could see in my eyes I ain't playin. All he sees in your eyes is love and titty milk.

Y'all couldn't even teach the boy how to ride a bike all because he tellin you he's scared. I put him on the bike and taught him to ride in one day. So, what if he scared? Kids are 'posed to be scared; everything is new to them. They always gonna be scared; adults are still scared. Part of my job is to teach him how to get through the fear so he won't be some scary ass adult that's afraid to do anything.

He wipes water from his eyes.

"If you couldn't make the boy by yaself you shouldn't be raisin him by yaself, but that's what you want. If it wasn't for his grandparents still babying you till this day, you would have been forced to need my help, but because you got them, you think you don't need me. Now they afraid to talk to me cuz they afraid I'm gonna take him away. Y'all stupid as hell. But whatever. Maybe you don't need me; clearly, you don't. You won't hear too many lil boys sayin they miss their dads, but you will see those same lil boys missing their smiles in every pic. Clearly, they missin something, they just afraid to tell you. But I'm over forcin myself in people's lives that don't want me there!"

"My bad, water is like a damn tape recorder; same thoughts every day. I send you my love and appreciation." His energy flows to the water, *bzzzt* the energy flows back to him. "*Thank you,*" he said smiling, as his body gyrates. His eyes roll back as he sits on the shower floor. His lips pucker up, and he kisses the air. Energy flows up his spine and into his head. The sound of a bone cracking can be heard coming from his skull. "*I wonder if my camera's audio can pick that up,*" he thinks. Euphoria flows throughout his body, prompting his lips to widen in a toothy smile. His hands come together as though in prayer, and he performs a sequence of mudras as if from Dr. Strange comic book. The perfect symmetry of his hands is mesmerizing. His pupils remain absent as the water bounces off his body. Finally, his pupils return, and he stops and turns off the shower.

As he's getting dressed to leave, his phone rings. "Yoooo," the voice on the phone says.

"What's poppin?."

"Ayye you talk to Kwame?"

"Now that I think about it, he ain't been answerin the phone."

"I'm bout to tell you som'n, don't say nothin. Nah, fuck dat, i'on care if you say somethin."

"I'm listenin"

"You know his girl be trippen right? He said he got into it with her because when you was over there at some point, you started singing, 'secret lovers.'"

"Nigga what? You bein serious?"

"Yes, the nigga said you was singin secret lovers, and I guess Tasha was on his ass like you was tryin to clown her to her face. She musta felt some kinda way about it."

"Like she thinks we're secret lovers? hahaha" D snorts a little. "I was singing secret lovers? Huh. I don't really remember doing that. But what if I was singing that? *Are we 'secret lovers'*? That seems like an easy 'shut the fuck up moment.' We not gay."

"Well, he was actin like he didn't know why you was singing that either."

D-Wood chuckles hard. "So, I'm the gay homie now? Now I'm suspect cuz I was singing secret lovers? I honestly don't know why I would be singing that, either," he says, confused.

"He didn't say you was gay. He said he didn't know why you was singin that."

"He knows we not secret lovers! Why he actin like he don't know that?" He asks, amused.

"I don't know, but I gotta go. I just got to the crib, and Ion want my wife to know I be hangin out witchu gay ass niggas." They both crack up at that.

"Fuck you! Ama holla back."

D-Wood walks out of the studio apartment.

"*It's Yahusha, not Yahshua, you idiot!*" yells a neighbor.

"What the hell they talkin bout?" mutters D-Wood as he walks up the apartment sidewalk.

He gets to the parking space where his car should be and pauses. He looks left and right before turning around and scanning the parking lot.

"Aaaaahhhhhh," he screams.

D-Wood sits on the couch as a dark-skinned buff black guy walks in the front door wearing a muscle shirt reading, *"Poppa Pump."*

"Wheres your car at? I thought you was gone," says Bo.

"They took my shit!" he replied, unamused.

"For real? Daaaaamn."

"Yeah, they caught me slippen! My camera and phone was in the car, and I was supposed to film this Art battle tomorrow. This some bullshit!"

"I can take you up there to get it."

"It's Fucking Friday!"

"Oh yeah, you can't get that back till Monday; you assed out!"

"Hell yeah, I was sleepin in my car."

"Why was you sleepin in ya car? You know I woulda let you stay here."

"Yeah, I know, but I couldn't really afford to give you that lil bit of money, and I didn't mind sleepin in my car. I just needed a place to shower."

"Well, you can stay here for a lil bit; you just gotta rub my back and wash my feet when I ask."

D-Wood cracks up. "This nigga just called me gay, now you askin me to rub yo crusty, stankin ass feet?!"

"Who called you gay nigga?"

"I'on wanna talk about it!"

Bo's face gets serious, and he looks D-Wood directly in his eyes.

"So... you rubbin my feet or nah?"

They both crack up.

"I fuckin hate you!" says D-Wood.

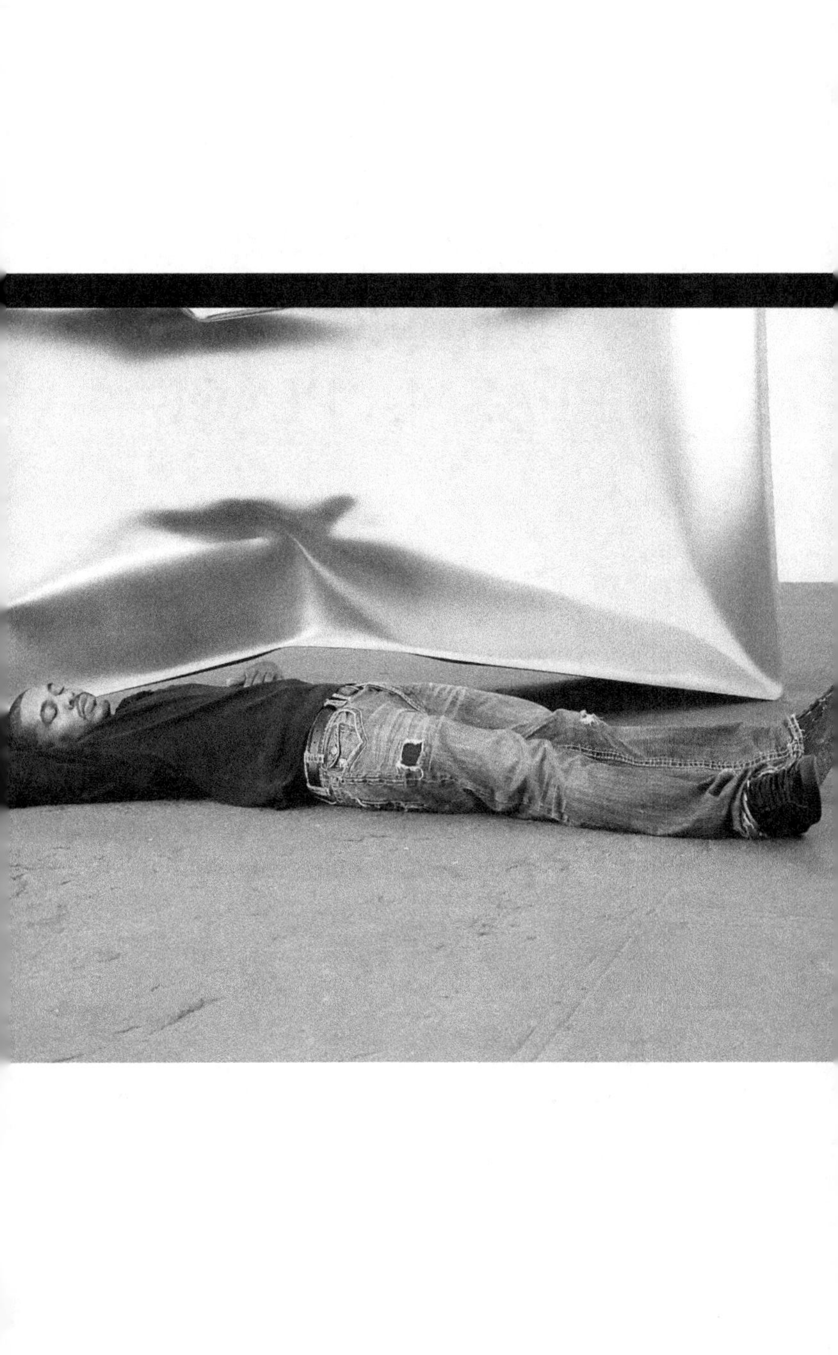

Chapter Sixteen

THANK YOU PLASMA PLACE

D-Wood watches a hairy-legged man in tiny jean shorts and a black T-shirt vigorously rubbing his hands together as he waits in a cubicle next to him.

"I know you burnin yo ass cheeks every time you sit in the car," says D-Wood looking at the man's shorts.

"I got Abe Lincoln's face branded on my ass right now from sitting on a penny!" D-Wood laughs as a chunky Hispanic woman appears in a white coat from behind a glass window.

"I'm sorry, you can't donate today. Your blood pressure is too low; it must be at least 80 over 50."

D-Wood stares back at her blankly.

"Do you want me to get a manager?" he shrugs.

She walks off and returns with another Hispanic co-worker.

"Si Senor, I see your blood pressure is too low. I'm sorry, we cannot let you donate today."

"CHECK (Clap) MY (Clap)

Blood (Clap)

PRESSURE (Clap)

NOW (Clap)

It's all the way up!"

"I'm sorry, we can't check it more than twice," says the manager.

With a tight lip, D-Wood turns around. He comes across an Asian man in a Dragon Ball Z shirt as he makes his way towards the exit.

"Are you Wu-Tang lan on the networks?" The guy smiles and nods. D-Wood's eyes widen in delight.

"I knew that was you!" says D-Wood smiling back.

"Was that racist?" he thinks to himself as he walks out the door.

Cheap perfumes, beers, and tobacco smoke encircled a dive bar. A Caucasian man dips a wing in his sauce. He takes a mouthful and looks at D-Wood unamused as he speaks into a microphone.

"Where my single people at?"

"Right here!" yells a blond woman.

"Y'all wanna know where I take women on the first date?" He looks at the audience, "I promise y'all participation trophies at the end of the show. I said, do y'all wanna know where I take women on the first date?"

"Where?" yells a few members of the audience.

"To donate plasma," he pauses and stares at the audience.

"Ask me why? Go ahead, ask me."

"Why?" yells a woman.

"Because the plasma place won't let anyone donate a second time if they have HIV or Hepatitis. So, if they stop you from donating on our second date, I'll know, baby...you're not the one." His contagious laugh causes more laughter from the audience.

" One time, they took the girl into the office, and when she came out, she didn't even say nothin to me; she just left. I said, thank you, Plasma place!" He puts his hands together as if he's praying.

"Cuz if they don't want her, guess what? I don't want her either. I'm tired of playin 'Russian Roulette' with these dirty heifas. I hate wearin condoms cuz as soon as it hits my penis, it shrinks like 'Mario' when the enemy hits him. I even hear the same sound as the video game, *'Bloomp. Bloomp. Bloomp.'* That sound is never good."

One lady in the audience bursts into wild laughter.

"Thank you, one lady who laughed," he says.

"Anybody meditate in here?"

One person raises their hand.

"I meditate; when I was younger, I used to pray, but meditation brings me more peace. When you talk to God, you gotta be careful what you wish for cuz you might just get it. I prayed for a bigger Penis, and I got it. The girth you receive from Gonorrhea is amazing." He pauses while the audience laughs.

"Turns out Gonorrhea is the only effective penis enhancer. This whole time, turns out dirty vagina can improve your girth in 24 hours. Clap if ya like girth, ladies."

A few ladies and one guy clap.

"I said ladies," he eyeballs the one man clapping, the audience laughs.

Chapter Seventeen

NOW I'M SUSPECT

In the driver's seat of a white Impala is a dark-skinned black man with locks. Kwame sits in the passenger seat while D-Wood sits behind the passenger seat. Kwame hands the driver a blunt.

"Tee, I'm still tryin to figure out why this nigga in the backseat was singin '*secret lovers*' at my house the other day."

The man smiles and looks back at D.

"Ooooh," says D-Wood, super hyped up.

"I been waitin for you to bring this shit up! Who gives a fuck if I was singin '*secret lovers*?!' Are we gay, Kwame?"

Tee looks at Kwame, holding back his laughter.

"Hell nah!" says Kwame

"Have I ever hit on you? Have I ever caressed you softly like a hoe? NO! It's one thing for your girl to be confused about the whole thing, and I wouldn't blame her at all. But how the hell YOU gon be confused? YOU shoulda told her to shut the fuck up soon as she suggested we could possibly be gay, because you know it as facts that we not."

D cracks up after the last sentence. "How did she manage to convince you that we could be secret lovers? This the most suspect shit I (clap) EVER (Clap) HEARD (Clap) NIGGA!"

Holding back laughter, Tee continues watching.

D-Wood looks at Tee,

"Can I smoke with you, or gay niggaz can't hit your blunt?" Tee hands him the blunt and bursts out laughing.

"Well, that shit was still suspicious," says Kwame.

"Arf. Arf. Arf." a tiny Yorkshire Terrier runs by the car barking.

"Shut up, Mimi," Kwame's girl yells from inside the house.

D-Wood sees the dog and has a flashback:

"Secret Loooooooovers, yeah, that's what we are." The Yorkshire Terrier clings to his legs as he sits on the couch.

"Ahahaha, OH SHIT! I know who I was singin *'secret lovers'* to."

"Who?" says Kwame

"Ya fuckin DOG! Because every time I visit your house, you act all weird when I pet your dog. Every time I pet your dog, you yell at it like it's doing somn wrong."

"No, I don't," says Kwame.

"The hell you don't! I still don't get why you be actin funny over your lil punk-ass dog." D looks at Tee and says, " I be pettin this niggas dog in secret whenever he go upstairs. He yells at the dog errytime he see me pettin it. Like his lil ass posed to be a guard dog."

Tee looks at Kwame,

"You do be actin weird bout your dogs. You won't let me see your other dog, and I got it for you."

"WHAT?!" says Kwame in a high-pitched voice. "Man fuck y'all. And don't sing to my fuckin dog no more. That's *my* dog!" They all crack up.

Chapter Eighteen
POKER FACE

D-Wood walks off an elevator into a law office in downtown Phoenix.

"May I help you?" asks the receptionist.

"Yeah, I have a ten-thirty appointment with Mrs. Wells."

The lady points to an area,

"Please have a seat over there while I give her a call." While sitting, he looks at the notes on his cell phone and whispers to himself,

"Listen more than you talk, listen more than you talk!"

"Collect call from Larry Wayne," said a voice in D-Wood's airpods.

"Do you accept?"

"Ayyyye, what's poppin?"

Dwood's eyebrows scrunch as a dark-skinned woman in business attire struts by.

"In this law office,"

Head facing forward, his right eyeball follows the woman-like booty detection software.

"Lookin at these yams out my peripheral."

"You ain't gone holla."

"You know I ain't got no game, my game be like,' I was gone talk to you yesterday. But you ain't comb your hair. But you combed it today, so...,"

they both chuckle.

"You stupid as hell, wussup with ya lil mans?"

"I ain't even been seein him since all this started. His momma gone tell me he's scared of me."

"Scared of you? Of course, he is scared of you. You, his daddy, he posed to be scared of you. "

"Member how you was when you started getting hair on ya nutts. And you started thinking you was hard."

"Matter fact, member, how we used to sell news-papers?"

"I ain't sell newspapers; I sold weed," says Larry Wayne, snickering.

On a Midwest Sunday morning in Des Moines, Iowa, wet leaves covered a driveway as a nineteen eighty-four blue Cutlass Sierra pulled into a neighborhood driveway at dawn.

Slam! Twelve-year-old D-Wood bangs a car door shut.

"Oh hell nah! Don't you be slamin my mothafuckin door. Is you crazy!" A young black woman yells in the driver's seat. Her tongue sucked over a gold tooth as she removed a toothpick from her mouth.

"You making me quit!" said D-Wood in his high-pitched voice.

"You think I'm wakin up at five am every day to take your ungrateful ass to deliver some newspapers; you out yo damn mind!" she said as she got out the car.

His hands were quivering, his big lips thinly mashed together as if they were being forced open.

"I hate you!" He mumbled, staring at the ground, balling his little fist.

"Fuckin Bitch!" He whispered to himself as he picked up a newspaper.

"What!"

The sound of leaves shuffled as a red blur appeared before him.

Boom! A violent, stiff jab compressed D-Woood's chest like a pickle top.

"Uhh," like a broken piñata quarters, dimes, nickels, and pennies jingled on the concrete.

"Forget soldier boy; I'm the first to have sonic coins knocked out his chest! And do you think I ever talked to her like that again?"

"Hell nah, and I bet yo daddy beat yo ass."

"She ain't even tell em; think about it. He used to wake me up and whoop my ass for no reason."

"Oh you was finna die die"

"I was gone be dead dead; why that sound like a hook?

"They said he had to die die, now that nigga dead dead."

Without missing a beat, Larry Wayne chimes in,

"Said you was hungry, and your daddy fed you lead lead."

"Came home, lil boy, what you said said."

"Take off all yo clothes, lay down on that bed bed."

"Boom Bang Pow..."

"Who you talkin' back to now!"

"Boom, Bang, Bip..."

Bring me the remote, for I empty out a clip."

"Ayyyye," D-Wood shoulders go up and down to a beat.

"Nigga you gotta remember they white, they call the man Father or Dad. We call our Dad Pops cuz if you act up, he gone Pop yo ass."

"And if you never been popped by your Pops, how you gonna act when you come across the cops."

"Bars"

"You have two minutes left," said an operator's voice.

A middle-aged blond woman walks up,

"I gotta go," he hangs up as she approaches.

"It's a pleasure to meet you, Mr. Chatwood. She smiles and extends her hand." He extends a handshake while maintaining eye contact with her.

"Good to meet you as well."

"As I stated in my email, I have the assistant Chief of Police with his advisors here to speak with you. We will discuss what happened and go from there."

D-Wood and the Defense Attorney walk into a room with two people sitting at a long table.

"Hello, I am Chief Kurtenbach, Assistant Police," one of the two says.

Another older woman steps forward and says, "I'm Maggie. I'm here as a witness."

"And you already know me," says the defense attorney.

They all sit down. Mrs. Wells speaks first.

"Would you like to give a brief opening statement, Mr. Chatwood?"

"I'm representing myself without an attorney, so I'm here to listen more than I am to speak; my complaint already says what happened."

He looks at the Assistant Chief of police,

"Have you seen the video?"

" Yes, I have, and let me start by offering an apology on behalf of the Phoenix police department. That may not go very far, but I want you to hear it from me at least."

"That's good to hear," D replies. The Assistant Chief continues,

"I want you to know that I support our officers wearing body cams, but we have not yet adopted this policy."

"Ooooh, they know they fucked up," D thinks without batting an eye.

Defense attorney Mrs. Wells speaks,

"In your damages, I read that you were diagnosed with PTSD. Are you on any medications?"

"Yes, I am. That information was included in the MIDP I sent, which contains my diagnosis and medications." She looks in her folder,

"Mmmhh, I can't find it here, so I'll check my email and print it. I'll be right back. " She leaves the room.

D looks at the Assistant Chief of Police,

"I do have one question for you."

"Shoot," he replies.

"Wasn't the police officer supposed to say something to me before tackling me to the ground? I still don't get why he didn't give me a chance to comply?"

"Yes, I'm unsure myself. But he definitely should have said something before using force. I want you to know we are doing our internal investigation and will have someone contact you, so please respond.

Do you have a phone number that I could have them call?"

"No, I don't have a number you can call at this time. I can only be reached through email. I'll reply within 24 hours," says D-Wood.

The defense attorney comes back in the room holding papers.

"Okay, I got it. We have a question for you, what do you want from this?"

D pauses, then says,

"I want to help stop this from happening to other people. So, I figure if I make a complaint, maybe it will show up on his record and stop him from doing it again. I'm lucky I was able to be calm in the situation. He could have gotten me killed if I had fought back, even though I would have been well within my rights to fight back because he didn't have a right to put his hands on me for no reason."

The defense attorney looks at the Assistant Chief of Police,

"Do you still want to move forward with what we talked about?"

"Yes," he replies.

The Defense attorney continues,

"After considering the circumstances, we are prepared to offer you a settlement of twenty-five thousand dollars."

"*Give me my money, BIIITCH!*" D-Wood screams in his head.

With no emotion, he replies.

"Okay, when would I need to answer if I would accept this?"

"If you could have an answer by next week, that would be perfect."

"I'll think about this over the weekend and get back to you next week."

D-Wood walks out of Phoenix City Hall calmly. When he gets through the door to downtown Phoenix he screams.

"AHHHHHHHH! BITCH!" An elderly Caucasian lady strolling by drops her cell phone on the ground. "My bad, lady!" He yells as she nervously picks it up.

With each word, he humps the air,

"THAT'S (*hump*)

WHAT (hump)

THE HELL (hump)

I'M (hump)

TALKIN (*hump*)

BOUT (*hump*)

BITCH! (*hump*)

AAAAHHH!"

He ponders at the bright blue sky,

"Spirit guides, y'all did ya Mu...fuckin thang! Okay, okay, y'all was right. You said go to the therapist!"

His shoulders get to moving as if he hears a beat in his head,

"Who got PTSD?" (clap clap) "I got PTSD?!" (Clap. Clap) "Who got PTSD?" (Clap. Clap). "I got PTSD, ayyyyye!"

He stops and contemplates,

"Should I accept the settlement? It's the first offer; why should I accept the first offer? Maybe I should hold out for fifty thousand?"

Bzzzzt, he vibrates, and a voice says,

"Do not accept the offer."

His shoulders slump down,

"Y'all get on my nerves," he says, annoyed.

"Fiiiine, I won't take it."

Chapter Nineteen

STUD TRIED TO GET ME FIRED

A Lox song, *Money, Power, Respect,* plays faintly as D and Kwame sit in a parked car. Kwame's eyes widen as they take shots from a shooter of Tequila and nod their heads to the music.

"Nigga! Do you know why I have to send my sister some money for a plane ticket? Some nigga left her stranded in Miami!"

"What? He canceled the ticket?"

"Hell yeah, cuz she ain't wanna give up no cheeks."

"Why would she go if she wasn't given up no cheeks?"

"Cuz she slow."

D-Wood looks over at Kwame with a serious face.

"Guess what I did when a girl flew me out once and told me to drop the draws? I dropped the draws, it just felt right."

"It just felt right? Shut the fuck up." Kwame burst out laughing. "You talkin 'bout that stud that flew you out?"

"She wasn't no stud. She was bald headed" D-Wood laughs.

"Yo, did I tell you how a stud tried to get me in trouble when I was a supervisor at my last job?" D-Wood asks.

"Ion think so," responds Kwame taking another gulp of beer.

"This is another reminder of how hate always backfires."

Wearing a lime-green collared shirt and tie, D-Wood sat at his work desk. A quote on a card pinned to his desk read,

Happy birthday, Boss, Don't ever change! We love you!

Bzzzt. D-Wood opens his desk drawer, picks up his vibrating cell phone, and reads a text.

"So, I heard you were asking about my relation-ship?"

He replies to the text, puzzled.

"Why would I be doing that?"

"Idk, but Lupe told me you were asking about me."

D's mind flashes to him sitting in the passenger seat of a black jeep, smoking a blunt with a fellow super-visor named Lupe.

" I love their lesbian relationship," says D-Wood. "Every time I'm on break, I always see Mya's girl-friend opening the door for her. I be like, 'aww, that's so sweet; she's the man of the relationship.' But then again, it's 350° degrees in the car, and she makin her get in first. Is that really sweet? Or is she trying to kill her on the low?" They both laugh.

"What if I'm talking to her girlfriend, and she's just fishing for info on some jealous shit."

He gets up and moves toward Mya, who slams her desk drawer shut as he approaches.

"Hey," says D, "Am I ...talkin to you?"

She smiles and nods,

"I'll be happy to help you with that."

She begins typing on her computer. D turns around, mystified.

"I thought she was gay," he muttered.

"Her fine ass better stop talkin to me, I know that!"

He gets another text,

"I was actually hoping you were asking because you liked me."

A huge smile comes over his face.

Later that day, D pulls into a QT gas station and pulls up to a grey SUV. As the window goes down, he sees Mya smiling at him. D-Wood yells,

"I'm gonna go get a blunt wrap, and then I'll follow you."

"Cool," she replies.

He comes out of the gas station and gets in a Silver Chevy Impala. Mya makes a quick exit from the parking lot. "Daaamn chicka!" he mutters as he pulls out after her.

As she turns the corner, her tires squeal.

"She think she Baby Driver? What da hell?" he thinks as his tires squeal too. A sign says the speed limit is 35 miles per hour, but his speedometer says he's going 56.

"She gotta be going like seventy; what the hell is wrong with her?"

She pulls into a parking lot, drives to the back, and gets out as 'Nine pm' flicks off his car radio. Avoiding eye contact, Mya looks around the park while he stares at her through his driver's window. D-Wood shuts his car door, but pauses.

"I keep comin back to my car, and my lights are on," says D-Wood, as his car light flicks off.

They walk towards a park bench beside an empty dog park.

"Sorry I was driving like that, but I had to make sure no one was following us," says Mya as she sits on a park bench.

"You got a stalker?" asks D-Wood.

"My ex drove by that gas station we just left." Mya's eyes widen as she takes a blunt out a Swisher sweet box. "She did that thing with your hands." Maya pointed two fingers at him, then back at herself.

"Oh shit, did she see me?" He asked, laughing nervously.

"I don't know, I think so."

"You called her your ex. Y'all break up?"

"Yeah, we broke up the other day." Mya flicks a bic and runs the flame up and down the blunt.

"I had to get out of that shit; too much arguing every damn day. So, you remember when you gave me my review, and I sat at your desk?"

"Yeah," D responds while tugging at his chin hair.

"She got all paranoid, acting like we were messin around."

"We don't ever talk; that was the most words we ever said to each other."

"I KNOW!" yells Mya.

Their eyes meet.

"I always thought you were cute, but I was never gonna holla at you. I assumed you were a full-blown carpet-muncher."

"Well, you assumed wrong!" she responds, smiling.

D-Wood coughs, then scrunch up his face.

"So, you're trying to tell me your ex put it in your head that I liked you, and that's why you texted me?"

"Yeah, I had to find out if it was true," his left eye-
brow raises.

"Talk about hate back firin."

The next day

"Ass ass ass ass," a song plays in one ear as D-Wood
walks through a call center.

"Synchronicity," he thinks, smiling as he examines
three gorgeous bottoms in his peripheral vision.

"Oweeeee," he thought as he eventually looked directly at a few ladies standing at a copy machine. As
he approaches the machine, he notices a girl stands
by his desk waiting on his arrival.

*"Why are people already at my desk? Can I sit
down before y'all start hounding me?"* he thinks,
passing an open office.

"MR. CHATWOOD!" yells a grey-bearded Caucasian man; "Please come see me." D-Wood smiles
at the girl standing by his desk and waves bye, as he
walks into the office. She rolls her eyes picking up a
folder.

"Have you heard of this guy?" He turns his lap-
top so D-Wood could see. A Caucasian man with
an afro is painting on YouTube, "I fucking love this
guy," says the bearded man smiling.

"I don't know who that is," says D-Wood. The
man turns up the volume and in the most pleas-
ant voice, the painting man says;

"We don't make mistakes; we just have happy accidents."

D smirks at the video.

"Happy accidents, I like that."

The man walks around his desk, shuts the door, and closes the blinds.

"So, how was Mya?" D-Wood pauses trying to hold his astonishment.

"What?"

"You heard me, David; how was Mya?"

"What? What do you mean?" The man returns to his seat smiling.

" I attended a meeting this morning. Can you guess what was discussed in the meeting? I'll just tell you; YOU! it was about you and Mya!" D's eyes widen.

"What? Are you for real?"

"Her girlfriend on Lupe's team went to Lupe and told her that you were messing with her girl-friend."

"Woooow," says D.

"You're not in trouble, so you don't have to worry about that. I'm just curious, how was it?" A mischievous grin spreads across the bearded man's face.

"I haven't hit it, man. I only hung out with her one time. She told me her ex saw us at the gas station.

We smoked a blunt, and that was it. Yesterday was the first time I hung out with her!"

"She's cute; you better hit that!" D-Wood's head cocks to the side, and he smiles.

"Ayye, she's nice! And I just broke up with my ex. But on the real, I haven't hit that. I ain't even kissed her."

The man looks unconvinced,

"Mmmmhhhh, well, I just wanted to give you shit; you're not in trouble. I've never heard anything like this about you, so I'm not concerned. But I need to know when you hit it!

Kwame's head tilts back. So, the stud tried to get you fired?" Kwame asked laughing.

"Hell yeah, told my Boss I took her girlfriend." Kwame takes a bump of cocaine with a dollar bill.

"You did take her girlfriend!" He hands the dollar bill back.

"They already broke up!"

"Nigga you took her girlfriend, and I know you hit it!"

"Not yet! I don't just be tryna smash the first time I hang out with a chick."

Chapter Twenty
THE LAST DRAGON

D-Wood picks up the dollar bill and takes another bump.

"I don't even know if I can tell you this part; you gon look at me crazy."

"Shut *uuup*" says Kwame.

"Ight, so like I said, I didn't hit it for about two weeks. I'd go to her house, and we would just talk our asses off. We never watched TV, didn't even turn it on. We never even went on a date; we just met up at her house, smoked, and talked for about two weeks straight. I was super rambling because this was when the spiritual shit I be telling you about first started happenin."

D-Wood, wearing dark blue jeans and no shirt, laid beside Mya on a floor mattress. She gazes at a faint scar on his caramel-colored chest. She stops observing and turns away while she ashes a blunt.

She leans back on the bed; her nipples poked like icicles through her silk robe. Her athletic velvety soft legs give off a sweet and creamy fragrance. D-Wood pretends to sniff the air as he notices her body.

"Is that ... rice milk and cherry blossoms?"

Mya giggles,

"How the hell? What?"

D-Wood smiles as his eyes bat over to the vanity dresser where a body lotion sits with the words *'Rice Milk and Cherry Blossoms'* at the bottom.

His contagious laughter echoes through the studio as she pushes him back, laughing.

"I was going to say I heard you were a Dog, but that's a keen sense of smell, boy."

D gives his best DMX Dog impression,

"Grrrrrrrr arf arf arf," and attempts to bite her leg. She quickly pulls away, giggling.

He reached into his pants, and he could feel the tent rising, and it became painful. To create room, he adjusts his member and loosens his belt.

"I got a question," says D. "Don't get mad either."

"What?" she asks, smiling.

"Did you and your girl use strap-ons?"

"Nope!" she responds, unbothered.

"For real?" says D, surprised. "Interesting, no wonder you be dry humpin the hell out of me; that's yo shit. You be trying to scissor me to death, but I like it."

"You better like it!"

She grabs his face and kisses him passionately.

He squeezes her ankle, and his body begins to tremble as he caresses her leg. A force field of growing energy causes the hairs on his arms to stand.

"What the hell is that?" he thinks as his hand parks over her warm apple pie like a hoverboard.

The palm of his hand tenses up.

"Oh my God," she whispers,

"Oooooh shit," says D, as they both experience tremors of ecstasy

"I'm not even touching her," he thinks.

They both stop moaning but continue panting as he takes his hand away. He returns his hand to her yoni, still unable to believe what has just occurred.

The energy returned like a reconnected battery.

"Whooooooooa," they moaned in unison.

"Ooooooooooooooooh shit." D-Wood takes his hand away,

"Did you feel that?"

"Uh yeah, I felt that," she says, perplexed.

Silence overcame them both; they stared at nothing for about a minute. Then, with a baffled face, he says,

"Umm, has that ever happened to you before?"

"No, it hasn't."

"You know I wasn't even touching you, right?"

"I know you weren't touching me, but I felt it."

"It's like we had an orgasm without ejaculating; that shit was crazy!"

Kwame takes another sniff of cocaine and casts a doubtful glance towards D-Wood.

"Oh, so you the Last Dragon now?" They both start singing in unison,

"You are the Last Dragon; you possess the power of the Glow Glow Glow Glow," they both cackle.

"Shut the fuck up!" says D. "I'm bein serious; this really happened! Energy was comin out of my hands and shit. It could be because she made me wait so long to hit, so our energies were hella intensified. I don't know; it hasn't happened like that with anyone else but her. Most girls just want to smash right away, so we don't build up like that. Or maybe, ...I don't know."

"So why did you stop messin with her?" says Kwame.

Chapter Twenty-One
ACRYLIC NAILS

Sweat flows down D's back as Mya's legs are wrapped around him like noodles on a fork. Bernie Mac's voice is playing in his head.

"Stir it like... muthaphuckin coffee; stir it like... muthaphuckin coffee." He makes a circular motion with his shaft each time he says to stir.

"I'm cumin!" she gasps. Her fingernails dig deep into his back. After she climaxes, D pulls out, and she looks at him, disappointed.

"I swear you never cum."

"What, you tryna get prego?" says D standing up. "You ain't on birth control; you'll be prego if I cum in you, that's a fact."

He walks naked to the bathroom to wash up. He feels a sting coming from his back; he checks in the mirror and notices three faint red lines going down his back.

"Gotdamn," he mutters. "I was doin my thang thang!"

He walks back into the room. Mya lights a blunt, her nipples poking unapologetically through her gold-gilded long lace robe.

"Look what you did to my back," he turns around, reaching towards the faint red scars.

"I didn't do that; it must have been one of your other hoes."

His head tilts back as he laughs out loud. He stops when he notices that she is not laughing with him. "You trippen; you literally just did this to my back!"

"Nope, I did not do that, I do not do that!" she replies, annoyed.

D thinks in his mind, *"Is she serious? Let me think... no, no hell no!"*

"You did this!" He covers his mouth, forcing himself to stop laughing as he can tell she is not amused.

HOW TO FIGHT A PIG

He grabs her and brings her close.

"My bad for laughin, but on errythang I love, I have not had sex with anyone but you; there is no one else that could have done this. That's why I'm crackin up."

She relaxes her eyebrows and hands him the blunt. D hits the blunt and thinks to himself,

"This bitch is crazy!"

Standing inside a Foot Locker looking at shoes; D answers his phone,

"Wudup." He says."I asked around, and acrylic nails do not leave a scratch. There's no way I could have scratched you nigga!" Mya says irritated. D looks at the phone eyebrows scrunched up,

"I don't care what you say; those are YOUR SCRATCHES," D says, emphasizing the latter part.

"Did this bitch just call me a nigga?" he thinks.

"I'm not gon do this with you, Daveed! Acrylic Nails don't leave a scratch; it's fuckin impossible!" yells Mya.

He looks at the phone, bewildered.

"Why in the world would I mention to you if another girl scratched me? That don't make no Gotdamn sense!"

"I don't fuckin know!" she responds.

"I'm hangin up!" D says annoyed and hangs up.

~❖~

Knock-Knock-Knock,

D-Wood stands outside of an apartment door. Mya answers the door holding a blunt; she turns around and walks back inside without a word.

"Look, I got proof that you did that to my back." He takes his shirt off and turns around, "Now look at the scratches. Notice how they scabbed over dark as hell now. Before, they just looked like three red marks because they were fresh."

She rubs over three parallel scratches.

"Close your eyes and rub it; It's like braille for blind people, and you know what it says? DON'T CALL ME A NIGGA IF YOU ARE NOT BLACK, and keep rubbin. It got another sentence it says ACRYLIC NAILS DO LEAVE A SCRATCH GOTDAMNIT!" he yells at her, frustrated.

Giggling, she says,

"I haaate you! You better not be lying to me!" she says while hugging him.

~❖~

Kwame takes a sip of beer,

"You musta been lustin over her ass to let her call you a nigga."

"Hell, nah, I didn't...Yeah, I did" D says, defeated. Then they both chuckle.

I ended up blocking her over that. She's a female; it ain't like I could beat the broad up. It ain't like the Police gonna let me off a domestic cuz she called me a nigga." D mimics a troubled voice," Officer, she called me a nigga. I didn't smack her; it was my ancestors." He laughs, picking up his beer.

Turning serious, he looks at Kwame and asks, "If I did catch a domestic, you ain't puttin no money on my books, is you? Nigga!"

"Hell, nah! I ain't," says Kwame laughing. "And stop frontin!" he continues, "I was *right there* in the back seat when the plug, a Mexican, was sayin all types of N words, and you ain't say *NADA*."

"That's different; he was putting money in my pocket," D says, shrugging.

"Well, pussy is a form of currency too."

"Oh, she put some pussy in ya pocket?" They both laugh.

"Nah, but callin me a nigga didn't really bother me. You wanna know what this broad said that really hurt my feelings? "

"What?"

"One day, I got to her house, and the first thing this winch said to me was, 'Chris Brown got a big ass dick.'" Kwame spits out his beer, laughing.

"Ain't that fucked up? I'm like, why the hell she tellin me this shit?"

"What you say?"

"I ain't say nothin; that's wussup. What the hell I'm supposed to say?" D's voice goes lower, "His dick ain't bigger than mine?"

"And she be like, 'Yeah, it is! Haha,'" says Kwame in a feminine voice.

"Now I got *'Chris browns dick,'* all in my search history."

"It *is* bigger, Fucking bitch!" says Kwame pretending to search the internet.

"I was lowkey offended, but we had bomb-ass sex. The only thing I think she didn't like is that I never came in her. I would always pull out."

"For what? See I'm gettin out the car. You always on that weird shit."

"See! This why I don't be tellin yo ass nothin. Soon as I wanna talk about somn real, you wanna get out the car. Make sure you take your punk ass gun with you and stop leavin that shit in my car witchyo scary ass!."

"Oh, yeah," Kwame reaches down and picks his gun off the floor. "Holla at me tomorrow," Kwame says and hops out. D puts his car in drive, cracking up, "Can't tell niggaz nothin!" he says pulling off the driveway.

Chapter Twenty-Two

LONG PISS: GOODNIGHT

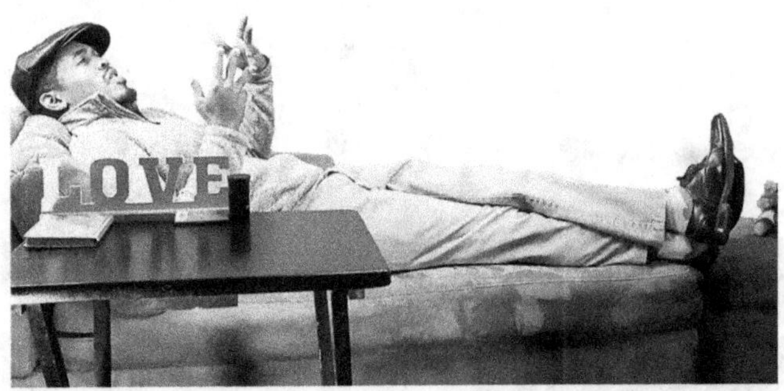

D-Wood sits on a comfortable leather couch, a plaque that said: *Anxiety and Depression Association of America* stands out on the wall behind him. An older Caucasian lady sits across from him while he speaks.

"I was born in Kansas City, Mo, but I first lived in Columbus, Ohio, with my Auntie, her husband, and my cousin. I remember when it rained, she would let us go out in swimming trunks and play in the rain. That used to be one of my favorite things. I do remember they had hella, I mean a lot of roaches. I could hear them slithering around when the lights were off.

"I don't remember transitioning from their house to me living in Des Moines with my Pops. My Pops tried to convince me that they took me to visit him around three years old, and I loved him so much I didn't wanna leave, but my Spidey sense told me that was a lie."

"Why do you think it was a lie?" says the Psychiatrist.

"Common sense. Most kids don't look at grown black men and think, 'I want to live with him.' Besides, my daddy looked mean as hell; ain't no way in hell I woulda volunteered for that. Dads are about discipline, moms are super soft and don't force you to do anything you don't wanna do. I'm pretty sure I went kicking and screaming, or my Aunt disappeared in the night after leaving me at his house, and I woke up sobbing like, 'Where's my Auntie?' and my dad was like, 'Shut up, boy, this ya new room, and that's ya new momma.'"

1990

"Aaaaaahhh, Daaaaady!" Eight-year-old D-Wood screams in panic from his bed. Everything was completely dark.

"I can't..." He put his hands to his eyes. "See anything!" he stammers, heart racing.

"*Ahchoo,*" snot flies out of his nose, covering his mouth as he sneezes. Still unable to see, he sobs as he wipes his nose with his hands and wipes them on the bed.

"What's wrong, David?" said a woman's voice.

"I can't see nothin," he tried to stand up.

Bing! He hits his head on the top of a bunk bed.

"Ooooh," he massages his forehead while crying out in frustration.

"Let me see ya eyes, baby. Open 'em up."

"I'm trying, but they won't open."

"It looks like they're glued shut."

"You been playin with glue?"

"No," he replies, sniffing.

"Just sit tight. I'll be right back."

He hears water running from the bathroom.

"What's wrong with the boy?" says a man's voice.

"I don't know; his eyes won't open up."

"His eyes won't open?"

"Ama put this warm towel over his eyes and see if that helps."

"It's prolly just his allergies. Warm up some milk in a shot glass, then put it over his eyes. He'll be alright."

The man scans his room,

"You better clean up this room or the next thing you gon see is me whoopin yo ass."

"Yeah," says D-Wood while holding the hot towel over his eyes.

Agitated, his father responds, "Yeah, what?"

"Yes sir," says little David in a small, high-pitched voice.

"Let me see," says the woman.

She puts two fingers over his eyelids and pulls. Slowly, his eyelashes unglue like food dried to a plate.

Before him is a black woman with a short Jheri curl. While she operated on his other eye, he admired her gold tooth.

"Oh my, your eyes are red and swollen as I don't know what. I ain't never heard of no warm milk going in da eye, but Big Daddy said it, so we gon do it, okay baby?"

"Yeah," he replied, happy to be able to see again.

1992

A fierce-looking, handsome, light-skinned man with a Jerry Curl, gold necklaces, and a grey suit swings down a belt. *Crack!* The belt snaps over the top of 10-year-old D-Wood's head. The boy's thick afro absorbs the blow.

Although he felt no pain, his body went limp. He collapses to the ground, screaming as though electric shocks raced through his body.

"Aaaaaahhhhh, you hit me in the head!"

With fire in his eyes, his father swings the belt over his shoulder.

"Leave the porch light on again! Take yo ass to your room and shut up!"

1993

Eleven-year-old D-Wood squints his eyes as he opens the curtains. The neighborhood is covered with a fresh layer of bright white snow. Sounding like a young Michael Jackson, he sings along to his favorite tv show, *Family Matters*.

> *"It's a rare condition*
> *this day and age*
> *to read any good news*
> *on the newspaper page.*
> *Love and tradition*
> *of the grand desiiiiiiign,*
> *some people say*
> *it's even harder to fiiiiiiiind."*

His father walks into the living room butt naked, holding a plate of food. His long shaft swings to a stop when he stops.

"I don't know what you lookin for; you better get out there and shovel it before it gets too heavy. Go grab two of them Hy-Vee grocery sacks out the cupboard, put one around each foot, then put another

HOW TO FIGHT A PIG

sock over the grocery sack so your feet won't get wet."

"Yes, sir," he responds, trying not to look directly at his dad's penis." He grabs two Hy-Vee grocery sacks from the cupboard and walks to his room.

"Why is he always naked, and why is his dick so big?" he thinks.

He enters his room and shuts the door behind him. He pulls his pants down and expresses dissatisfaction as he examines his penis.

"You better fuckin grow!" He pulls the knob on a small box TV in his room. The TV blasts,

"SECRET GROWTH DISCOVERY WILL IN-CREASE YOUR PENIS SIZE BY 3.61 CM PER WEEK!" He quickly lowers the TV's volume and grabs a pen and pencil.

"Call today and receive one box of red pills free." He writes down the phone number.

1994

Twelve-year-old D-Wood wakes up to the sound of the garage door opening. He checks his alarm clock, which reads 5:47 a.m. He hears the front door open and listens as the sound of jingling keys approaches his room, followed by the vibration of hard footsteps.

RIIIING! Their house alarm screams so loudly that it can be heard from blocks away.

"Gotdamnit!" says a man's voice. Little D listens attentively to jingling keys, and then the alarm stops.

Riiiiiiiiing! A house telephone rings, and a calm manly voice answers.

"Hey now, this is him, false alarm, the code is 4567; everything's good."

Clack. Clack, the sound of dress shoes hits the bathroom floor.

Crack, a toilet seat lid slams back. *Pssss ssssssssssssssssssssssssssssssssssssssssssss... psssssssssssssssssssssss... psssssssssssssssssssss.*

Young D-wood listens intently to the sound of urinating.

"How the hell does he pee for so long?" He thinks to himself. *Pssssssssssssssssssssssssssssssss,*

"Does he pee that long cuz his dick is so big? I hope I have to pee that long one day." The pee pauses then resume. *psssssssssssssssssssssss.*

"Every time he pees this long, he comes in here whoopin my ass." D-Wood rolls to his side, joins his hands, and begins to pray.

"Please, God, make him go to sleep," he says repeatedly.

He finally stops urinating. *Crack,* he hears the toilet lid slam down, and the toilet flushes. The sink water runs for a moment, then stops.

The shadow of a pair of feet appears below his sliding door; he quickly shuts his eyes tight and pretends to be asleep. He hears his sliding door open; he keeps his eyes closed but stops breathing.

His father stands before him with lion eyes, a pimp's attire from the 70s, gold jewelry around his neck, and multiple rings that could puncture your forehead.

Little D doesn't move an inch, but his mind races.

" Okay, I took out the trash. He just came out of the bathroom; did I clean the bathroom? Did I remember to turn on the porch light? Did I clean my room before I went to bed? Please, God, tell me my room is clean!"

After examining the room, the man looks at his son, his body still as a mannequin, but his eyeballs slightly move behind his eyelids.

" You gon breath lil boy?" Little D doesn't respond.

"You a bad actor," his father says as the phone rings. He walks out of the room and shuts the sliding door. Little D smiles as his shoulders go up and down. In his mind, he starts singing one of his favorite Tv shows.

"It's all right, cuz I'm saved by the... it's all right cuz I'm saved by the... it's all right cuz I'm saved by the bell." He does a guitar riff with his hands under the cover and turns over.

He is startled by a loud yell from his father's room,

"DON'T YOU COME OVER HERE UNLESS YOU GOT MY MOTHAFUCKIN MONEY!"

D thinks to himself,

"Please come over so he can leave me the hell alone."

"Lil Boy, I know you awake in there."

"*What I do now?*" thinks D.

He gets up and walks to his father's bedroom.

"Yes, sir," says his tiny high-pitched voice.

"There are some Pancakes from *Shoney's* in the kitchen; better get it while it›s hot.» Little D›s face lights up,

"Yes, sir, thank you."

~❖~

Little D sits on a bottom bunk bed in his room and observes a bottle of red pills with disappointment as the Midwest sun brightens the room. The snoring sound of a Grizzly Bear comes from the other room.

"*They said my dick would grow after two weeks; I should get my money back!*" He looks down at his penis. "*Ain't no way in hell I'm gon call them and say my dick still small, and I want my money back!*"

He does a quick shake-and-bake move treating the pill bottle like a basketball.

"Three-two-one," he shoots the Pill bottle into the garbage.

He walks back over to the trash can and takes the bottle out.

"I'm *gettin my money back*," he thinks.

He takes the bottle and tiptoes through the hallway. The sound of the grizzly bear grows loud as he tiptoes past his dad's room.

He gets to the front room and stops,

"I don't know if he turned off the alarm." He looks up at a white box above the kitchen.

Mission impossible music started playing in his head. He get's on his belly and starts shuffling towards the kitchen. He had learned the motion sensor could not detect him if he was low enough. Once in the kitchen he could stand up.

Finally, he picks up the phone quietly and dials a number.

A woman answers the phone,

"Thank you for calling Network Shopping; how can I help you?" Little D immediately gets nervous.

"*Why it gotta be a woman?*" he thinks, frustrated.

"Hello, I can hear breathing," says the woman.

Trying to sound like a man, he adds more bass to his voice.

"Umm, yes, I read I could get my money back if these pills didn't work."

"What pills did you purchase?"

In his regular high-pitched voice, he says,

"I bought the pills-" he stops abruptly and starts over in his man voice. "I bought the pills you sell."

"We sell many different pills, sir; what are they called?"

"*Why does it gotta be a woman,*" thinks D again.

"Hello, sir?"

"More inches"

"I have never processed a refund for that one; let me check. Oh," she says. "So, how long have you been taking these?"

"Over two months."

"I'm sorry to hear that. May I ask how old you are?"

"I'm twenty-two," says little D

"Okay, because I know these wouldn't work on a child; you sound a little young, sir."

"I'm old eno-" he stops because he hears an echo. "I'm old enough," he says again.

A man's voice interrupts,

"Old enough to do what? Boy, I'm gon beat yo ass! What is this? Phone sex? You orderin phone sex on my phone lil boy? Is this that, 'Pick up the phone shit?' Is this that, 'Pick up the phone shit?' Well, guess who done picked up the phone and bout to beat yo ass. You tryin to pay for some pussy, boy? Don't you know you don't pay for no pussy, pussy pays for us! Get off the mothaphuckin phone, so I can see who you talkin to."

D hangs up the phone; eyes watered up.

He can hear his father still talking on the phone.

"Who the hell is this?"

"He said he wanted a refund."

"For what?"

"Some pills."

"What kinda pills?"

"More inches?"

"More inches on what?"

"Say that again?"

"Buahahahaha,"

D listens to his father laughing, unsure whether it's good or bad.

"The boy said he wanted a refund, huh?"

"So, I guess it didn't work, huh?"

"So, is he gon get his refund?"

"The boy only twelve years old, prolly ain't even got hair on his nuts yet." He bursts out laughing. "You say you gon send his money back? Well, I'm his Daddy. I guess he tryin to get like me. You know his Daddy's blessed. Oh yeah. Well, go ahead, write my number down. And thank you for sending my boy his refund - the lil damn fool. Thank you." *Click*, he hangs up the phone.

"Oh, you a fool for the people, boy." His father laughs out hard. I thought you was talkin to one of those sex operators. If you want some pussy, I can get some for you, boy. Don't you waste no money on no more dick growin pills. Why you think you need pills to grow ya dick?"

With tears streaming down his face and his voice trembling; D-Wood says,

"Because you gave me them magnum condoms, and they too big, I can't fit em."

"You ain't supposed to be able to fit em yet, you twelve. I gave em to you, so you know you ain't ready to have sex until you can fit one, ya damn fool. Until then, sit ya lil dick ass down."

"Okay," says little D, sniffing.

A sound of snoring emanates from his father's room.

"This gon work, though," thinks little D in his bedroom. He picks up a string tied to a rock and looks over the yarn to ensure it is tied securely around the stone.

"If I do this every day for an hour, there's no way it won't grow."

He stands up after fastening the string to the end of his penis. Alarmed by the quiet, he freezes like a deer in the woods.

Argh, gak, gasp, the sound of a man coughing comes from a room, followed by grunts like a Wild Boar; *Zzzz,* the snoring starts again.

Exhaling, Little D struts around his room in circles as the stone hangs from his penis.

"Who dick bout to grow?" *Clap, Clap.* "My dick bout to grow." *Clap Clap.*

    HOW TO FIGHT A PIG

1997

Fifteen-year-old D-Wood stands sleepily with no shirt on, staring at his father. His Pops is wearing his usual pimp suit with hat attire.

He observes his father's mouth opening and closing but hears nothing. Instead, he heard homer Simpson's voice saying,

"Blah blah blah blah blah, blah blah blah, blah blah blah."

D glances at the clock; it's 5:24 am. He looks back at his father to see his red eyes glaring at him like a lion, ready to pounce.

"Ya lookin at me like you think you tough, Lil ugly mothafucka."

"How am I ugly if I look like you," thinks D.

"That's okay, I got som'n for ya ass." He roars, "AMA KILLAH, BOY!" D startles at the intensity of his thunderous voice. His father takes off his pimp hat, tosses it on the couch, and pulls out two leather gloves from the top pocket of his suit.

No, you're a murderer!" thinks D. "It's not even cold outside; what is wrong with him? *When they put on leather gloves in a movie, they bout to kill somebody."*

Bouncing like Muhammad Ali, his Pops puts on the black leather gloves.

"Oh yeah, I ain't OJ; my gloves fit."

He bounces around with a menacing grin,

"Put up ya dukes, mothafucka!"

Glaring back, little D prepares to defend himself. His Dad starts swinging, *Boom*-left jab, *Pow*-right jab. D dodges both punches. *Bang,* a right cross connects with a thud.

D-Wood stops to take a drink of water in the Psychiatrist's office.

"So, how is your relationship with your father now?"

"It's not the best; but I love my Pops. I got over that stuff a long time ago."

"How?"

"I knew he was the best father he could be. But, growing up as he did, you had to be tough. I think him kicking my ass all the time was his way of preparing me for the world. Of course, he could have done it sober, but some lessons don't come with a chalkboard; they come with a drunken fist."

LOVE

Chapter Twenty-Three
HONOR ROLL

"**D**id you always get beaten when you got into trouble?"

"When I think about it, it's prolly why I believe in Karma. Cuz even though I never got caught, I was always gettin a whoopin, but the one time I thought he would kill me, he didn't do nothin."

1999

Squeaking tennis shoes echoes across the gymnasium floor as D-Wood and five other teenage black boys play three-on-three.

The shortest of the group, E, has the ball. His defender jumps, falling for a pump fake. He crosses over and drives to the hoop for an easy lay-up.

"Oooooh," says D-Wood, face scrunched up, "That's game!"

After making the shot, the shortest homie bends his knees and starts humping the air,

"See my diiick," *hump hump,* "See my diiick," *hump hump.* In basketball shorts, he humps the air while looking at his penis. The remaining five glance at each other awkwardly.

The gym door opens, and a short, chubby Caucasian lady enters.

"I told you guys to stop coming in here after school!"

Before she could get three words out, all six ran through the nearest gym door. They run a few paces outside the door, then slow down to walk.

The lighter-skinned boy dribbling the basketball speaks with a loud voice that echoes across the field. The tallest boy stops walking, looks at the shortest with disgust, points his finger at him, and says,

"E, don't you ever do that bullshit again!" he says, face scrunched up.

"Do what?" he replies. The boy starts mimicking E,

"See my Diiick," *hump hump,* "See my diiick!" He looks at D-Wood and the others, "Y'all see him humpin the air all hard, you couldn't see nothin; it looks like a mu-fuckin heartbeat."

Spit flies out of D-Wood's mouth as he faints to the grass, dying of laughter.

"AAAHHHHH!" a high-pitched scream flies out of one boy's mouth. The other two bend over, laughing while holding their stomachs.

"I can't breathe," says D-Wood, still laughing hard. E's lips tighten up. D-Wood looks up from the grass, gasping for air.

"I was a lil uncomfortable." D says.

"Shut up, Eyebrows!" he glares at D-Wood. They all keep laughing like hyenas.

He looks back at the tallest boy,

"Get off my dick! This is high school, yet you wear that orange jumpsuit so much that Mr. Ruland calls you inmate 67983.

They all burst out laughing.

The light-skinned kid chimes in,

"He did try to pay me in a bag of chips and some beef jerky yesterday," he laughs

"Smellin like Febreze and no future," laughs D-Wood.

"Speakin of commissary," says the tall boy. "Look at his face, all them damn pimples! Forehead looks like a pop tart!

They all hold their stomachs laughing.

"You strawberry cream-filled biiiiiitch!"

Tommy mocks their laughter,

"That's okay; my dick is bigger than all of y'alls! Y'all can sing, 'see my dick, *hump, hump*, See my dick, *hump, hump*. And ama call y'all the *Five Heart Beats*," he points at the only one that hasn't said any-thing. "And Crackhead gon be Eddie Cane."

"At least, we can afford to get som'n to drink," says D-Wood. "Only time this nigga gets soda is when he asks for a water cup. Broke ass nigga, *'can I get some water? can I get some water?'* Ole water cup-ass NIGGA."

They all continue cackling.

A short mature male Asian teacher stands in front of a chalkboard.

"Take out your books and turn to page thirty-three."

He turns around and begins writing on the chalkboard.

In unison, twenty-five wadded-up paper balls fly at the teacher's back.

BAM! A wet paper towel slams into the chalkboard forcefully. D-Wood sits down quickly with his hands wet from holding the toilet paper.

The teacher doesn't turn around right away. He appears to be taking deep breaths as his shoulders raise.

BOOM! The teacher slams a thick Physics book into the ground with both hands. The sound echoes through the hallways like a gunshot.

"NO! NO!" he yelled, face red. The classroom's formerly rebellious atmosphere suddenly changes to fear.

"WOOD, YOU DO DIS TO YOUR FATHA! YOU RESPEK ME! LIKE YOU RESPEK YOUR FATHA!"

Knock knock knock; a student stood at the doorway.

"Yes," says the teacher.

"Mr. Lee, I have a pink slip for Da Da David Cha Chad Wick."

"It's Cha Cha Chat WOOD," says D-Wood grabbing the pink slip.

No longer in the teacher's eyesight, D-Wood stands outside the classroom door, dancing, humping the air, and laughing at the students.

"Mr. Chatwu!" yelled Mr. Lee. He takes off and runs towards the office. After turning the corner, he takes a few steps and stops abruptly.

"Damn," cries a boy, barely avoiding walking into him.

D-Wood stands staring like he saw the Texas Chainsaw Massacre.

He recognizes his dad's pimp hat from the hallway.

"What the hell is he doing here?" he thinks.

Mrs. Bruce spots him from the hallway.

"Come on in, Mr. Chatwood," she says, smiling.

D walks in, heart pounding.

"Yes, ma'am."

" We summoned your father because it seems Mrs. Hart, our hall monitor, cannot keep you and your buddies out of the gym after school. If one of you gets hurt there, the school will be held accountable, and we can't risk it.

"Yes, ma'am," says D-Wood

"Let them have to call me again about you sneakin in the damn gym," says his dad. "And I got ya report Card too." he lets out the most villainous laugh.

A lump forms in D's throat as his eyes tear up.

Two years earlier

After school, D Walks into the computer room, then walks to the teacher and asks in a sheepish, childish voice, "Mrs. Deskin, is it alright if I use the scanner?"

"Of course, you can use the scanner; you know what to do." She replies politely.

"Thank you," he replied.

With suspicion written all over his face he looks around the room. He pulls out an envelope after being certain that no one is looking. The teacher gets up, making his heart speed up. Then she walks out of the room.

"Thank God," he thinks. He reaches into the envelope, takes out a piece of paper, and places it face down on the scanner. He pushes the scan button nervously and walks to the back of the room. To prevent anyone from walking behind him, he sits at the chair farthest to the right. He then uses the mouse and hovers over a file. He right clicks and scrolls to the words, 'Open in paint.' His report card pops up on the screen.

Algebra	C
Biology	C
U.S. History	B

Computer Science	A
Physical Education	A
Foreign Language	B-
Art	B

He puts a square over the B, hits CTRL C to copy it, then CTRL V to paste, and the B reappears on the screen.

He drags the B and places it over the C in Biology. He hits CTRL V again, and the B reappears. Finally, he carries the B and puts it over the C in Algebra. He smiles, amazed at how flawless everything seems.

"Look who's back on the honor roll," he whispers. He saves the file then hits Print.

Smiling, D-Wood says, "I gave my Pops a fake report card from my sophomore to my junior year. He didn't want to accept a report card with any C's, so I wasn't gonna give him one. I was punished for almost six months when he found out, but it was worth it. He never even whooped me for that; I think he was impressed I even knew how to do it."

Chapter Twenty-Four
THE DEPOSITION

Vanilla folders are placed in front of D-Wood as he scoots closer to a long table. A blond Caucasian woman sits to his left, typing every word uttered. Sitting across from D-wood is the new defense attorney, a Ginger Caucasian man in his mid-thirties.

"So, they brought Bobby Axelrod from 'Billions' to play hardball," thinks D-Wood. *"No wonder they had to change attorneys. He looks like he ain't afraid to lie to win."*

"Would you like bottled water?" Axelrod hands D a bottle of water.

"Can't drink that," thinks D. He accepts the water and sets it away from him. He was on a dry fast and had not drunk nor eaten anything in 48 hours.

"Did anyone help you write your complaint?"

"No," responds D.

"How did you figure out what to put in your complaint?"

"I went to the Phoenix Law Library. "

"Where is the Phoenix Law Library?"

D pauses,

"Why is he asking that," he thinks. He points outside through the blinds. «You can actually see it from here; I could point you towards the building.»

"Is this something you have done before?"

"No. It took me two weeks, over eighty hours, to complete the complaint."

One hour later, he was still being questioned by the attorney. "When Glendale officers beat you up, did you take any time off work?" asks Axelrod

D pauses, *"I don't really remember,"* he thinks. «No,» he answers.

"If you didn't take time off work when you got beat up, why did you need to take off work for this?"

"Motherbastard," thinks D, *"I knew that was a set-up."*

"I don't know," he answers.

He looks down at a note written on a piece of paper. *'Don't answer if you don't know,'* says one line.

His face scrunches up; he looks in the air.

"Ooooooh snap, I was selling dope back then. I didn't have a job, so I didn't take off work." He strokes his chin hair. *"I think I'll just keep that to myself,"* he thinks. An hour passes, and D-Wood is still in the room with the attorney. A projector shows D-Wood's video of him being tackled by the officer. In the video, D-Wood walks to the first car he saw

in the accident, and he is heard saying to the people in the car,

'Y'all hear that? They actin like I did something wrong.'

Axelrod stops the tape,

"What did you mean by that?"

"I didn't actually hear any words, but the way the helicopter shone the light on me made me feel as though they were accusing me of something." Axelrod looks at David's water bottle after another hour, "Would you like to take a break?" he asks.

"Nope, I wanna get it done as soon as possible."

D looked at the bottle of water,

"Fuck yo water." he thinks.

"Okay," says Axelrod. "Well, what about the witness tape saying you were the wrong-way driver?"

"What? what tape? I haven't heard no tape saying I'm the wrong-way driver." Axelrod pushes play on a link. A man speaks,

"I see a black man in a grey sweater walking; I think he's the wrong-way driver."

D-Wood's face scrunches up. D thinks in his head,

"That's gotta be fake; how would anyone even know there's a wrong-way driver unless they saw the accident happen? I didn't even know that until I saw the police report." Then, after a long pause, D says,

"That doesn't make any sense."

Axelrod continues,

"If the officers think you are the suspected wrong-way driver, doesn't it give them a reason to make contact with you?"

D pauses,

"Yes, it makes sense that they would make contact, but it doesn't make sense that they would knock me to the ground without first warning. Making contact, in my opinion, means the officer announcing himself and issuing vocal directives first. But this officer just tackled me to the ground! I don't have a problem with officers making contact; I have a problem with them using excessive force."

D looks at his water and pushes it further away from him.

"The officer did give prior warning before tackling you."

D laughs genuinely hard at that. "Really? How will you guys say that after the officer already admitted in his response to the complaint that he did not give a warning before tackling me?"

"Did you see our amended response, where he said he gave a warning?"

"I saw it, and I thought it was hilarious. You can clearly hear what was said on the tape."

"Thank you for coming to the deposition, Mr. Chatwood; that concludes all of my questions for today. However, off the record, I would like to meet with you in another room before leaving if you have time. Is that possible?" asks Axelrod with a straight face.

"We can do that," D-Wood responds. He turns to the court reporter, "Have a good day."

"You too," she responds.

D-Wood and Axelrod walk to another smaller room with no windows; they sit across from each other.

"Man, he looks like Axelrod," thinks D-Wood. «He›s even eye-fucking me *as a guy does to people on the show; Ama stare right back at your ass too."*

"Okay, Mr. Chatwood, I'm being honest with you; I think I can win this in court. As a matter of fact, I'm confident I can win."

"I think I can win as well," D-Wood responds.

"We can go further and keep going back and forth; we still have a few more things to do before the trial in July. I note that the previous lawyer has already made you a settlement offer of twenty-five thousand, and I'm willing to maintain that offer. So, we can end this today or continue fighting for a few more months and see what happens."

"Mmmhh," D looks up, contemplating the offer.

"I sure as hell don't have no business trying to defend myself in court. Twenty-five racks is definitely enough for that weak-ass tackle. I'm really over this; it's been a whole year!"

He looks at Axelrod.

"What about thirty thousand?"

"I can't go over the twenty-five; it's pretty much our threshold for this type of case with your damages."

"All right, whatever, I'll take the twenty-five."

"Okay, I'll go get the paperwork for you to sign."

"Hold on, does this paperwork mean I can't talk about this?"

"No, you can still talk about it as much as you want. I'll go get it printed and bring it to you. Unfortunately, I won't be able to write the check today, but you should be receiving it within two weeks."

"Okay."

After D-Wood signed, Axelrod walks him to the elevator and shakes his hand.

"It was a pleasure meeting you, Mr. Chatwood."

"You too," Axelrod begins walking back towards his office and stops as D-Wood gets to the elevator.

"Mr. Chatwood," he yells; D looks back.

"Thank you for stopping!" D-Wood smiles,

"No, thank that officer for tackling me." Axelrod laughs as D gets on the elevator.

Wavy Folio

Chapter Twenty-Five
CULTURAL APPROPRIATION

It's Halloween at a comedy club. Speaking on stage is a heavyset Caucasian woman wearing a pink dress.

"Each comic is given four topics on which they have to write a three-minute set in 5 minutes. The first-round topics are Teenage Trick or Treaters, Colonoscopy, and Cat Toys.

"Our first comic coming to the stage with a little cultural appropriation is Wavy Folio."

D-Wood struts to the stage wearing an Indigenous outfit with a Chief Headdress. A Caucasian lady in the front row says, "How?" with a stereotypical Native American accent from old movies. A few people chuckle.

"How" he goes right into his set chanting. "Too many Indians, not enough Chiefs, if yo ass trick or treatin you gon get yo ass beat." The crowd laughs along with the judges, but he keeps going.

"Too many Indians, not enough Chiefs. Would you like a Colonoscopy for a treat? "More laughter.

He looks back at the wall, Cat toys was his last topic.

"Oh yeah, and what can I say about Cat Toys? That's usually what I stand by at the grocery store when I'm stealing food to eat cuz there ain't no camera over there. You can literally stand by the Cat toys and eat as many fresh vegetables and fruit as you want!" he laughs out loud at his own joke.

Chapter Twenty-Six

WHEN ACTING LIKE A PUNK GOES RIGHT

The Sun shines off an apartment window causing D-Wood to back his chair into the shade. A leafless tree occupies the center of a grassless yard.

D-Wood hands Kwame a black sack as he takes out a bottle of Ciroc.

"Oh shit, this what we doin?" says Kwame, "I thought you was broke, I seen ya facebook post with your sad ass bank account." Kwame says while laughing mockingly.

"Nah. I wanted to give anyone a chance to send me some money, so I wouldn't feel bad for not sending no one else no money. I finally got my CHECK NIGGAAAAA!"

"Oooh shit, you got it! How much you get?" says Kwame smiling hard.

"Twenty-five."

"Haha! Daaamn. You really did that shit!"

"Hell yeah! That complaint was the best thing I wrote in my whole life!"

"That's dope!" says Kwame.

"Now tell me I'm stupid for stoppin to help somebody, nigga!"

"You are stupid!" Kwame says with a laugh, "but you stupid with some monaay! And all you did was write a complaint?"

"It was more than the complaint. See, our problem is we so busy actin' hard, when sometimes you gotta act like a bitch to get some money."

"Here you go."

"Nah, I ain't even tell you what I did before I got the PTSD diagnosis."

"What?"

One year earlier

D-Wood gets out of his car inside a hospital parking lot. He takes a deep breath, holds it, and begins heading toward the ER entrance. *Whack*, he smacks himself. *Whack*, he strikes himself again. A vein pops out of his forehead, and he continues to hold his breath as he nears the entrance. His face is red as he walks through the lobby, and his steps slow down as he reaches the front desk.

"Can I help you?" asks a middle-aged Caucasian lady. D-Wood's voice grew thick and unsteady, "I... I'm having trouble... breathing. I don't know wha... what's ha... happening."

"I'll get you a nurse in a moment."

~❖~

Lying in a hospital bed in a gown, D-Wood talks to a nurse.

"I was driving on the 202 and thought I was getting pulled over, but the cops passed me. I couldn't catch my breath; it felt like I was running twenty miles at full speed. Then my feet began to get numb, making pushing the pedals with my feet increasingly difficult. But luckily, I knew I wasn't very far from this hospital, so I drove here."

"Do you have any reason to be afraid of the cops?" says the Nurse.

     HOW TO FIGHT A PIG

"I stopped at a car accident the other day, and on my way back to my car, an officer came out of nowhere and knocked me to the ground."

"Did they arrest you?"

"No, they let me go. Maybe it spooked me more than I thought it did."

"Sounds like you had a panic attack, I'll be back, and we will get you hooked up to an EKG." The Nurse leaves, and he begins to sing and giggle while bouncing his shoulders back and forth.

"Guess who had him a panic attack? I'm getting diagnosed with a panic attack!" A hand reaches through the curtains, and happiness wipes from his face like a makeup remover

Kwame is laughing hard now as D finishes his narration.

"I had to get a shot in my ass and everything," says D-Wood.

"So, it wasn't just the complaint letter; it was the mental damages of having a panic attack and being diagnosed with PTSD."

"You was in the therapist's office lookin sadder than a bitch." Kwame says, laughing hard.

"Hell, yeah. Scrap all that gangsta shit. We too busy trying to be hard after the police whoop our ass. We better get compensation like these white folks would do!"

A car pulls up as a hip-hop instrumental beat plays. D-Wood and Kwame start bobbing their heads. Then, D-Wood starts rapping to the beat.

"I'll show you how to fight a pig

Ya Dig?

I'll show you how to fight a pig

Ya Dig?

I'll show you how to fight a pig

Ya Dig?

Holla atchya boy I'll show you how to fight a pig

1983 lawsuit quick!

You ain't never heard of it

Cuz you been tricked!

Out of sight out of mind

They think they slick

They get away with so much

That it makes me sick

So if the popo did you wrong

You might benefit from this song

Look, put this in ya ear drum

Play it over and over

Tell ya ears, numb

You want some real knowledge?

Here it comes:

Forget about me

Don't matter where

You hear it from

Take out ya camera

Thats ya witness

Be calm and collected

That's ya business

I ain't tryin to tell you to be no punk

I just want you to win

If ya head gets lumped

Uh

I'll show you how to fight a pig

Ya Dig?

I'll show you how to fight a pig

Ya Dig?

I'll show you how to fight a pig

Holla atchya boy. I'll show you

How to fight a pig."

MERICA